THE SMARTEST MONEY BOOK YOU'LL EVER READ

Also by Daniel R. Solin

DOES YOUR BROKER OWE YOU MONEY?

THE SMARTEST INVESTMENT BOOK YOU'LL EVER READ

THE SMARTEST 401(K) BOOK YOU'LL EVER READ

THE SMARTEST RETIREMENT BOOK YOU'LL EVER READ

THE SMARTEST PORTFOLIO YOU'LL EVER OWN

THE SMARTEST MONEY BOOK YOU'LL EVER READ

*Everything You Need to Know
About Growing, Spending, and
Enjoying Your Money*

Daniel R. Solin

A PERIGEE BOOK

A PERIGEE BOOK
Published by the Penguin Group
Penguin Group (USA) Inc.
375 Hudson Street, New York, New York 10014, USA

Penguin Group (Canada), 90 Eglinton Avenue East, Suite 700, Toronto, Ontario M4P 2Y3, Canada
(a division of Pearson Penguin Canada Inc.)
Penguin Books Ltd., 80 Strand, London WC2R 0RL, England
Penguin Group Ireland, 25 St. Stephen's Green, Dublin 2, Ireland (a division of Penguin Books Ltd.)
Penguin Group (Australia), 250 Camberwell Road, Camberwell, Victoria 3124, Australia
(a division of Pearson Australia Group Pty. Ltd.)
Penguin Books India Pvt. Ltd., 11 Community Centre, Panchsheel Park, New Delhi—110 017, India
Penguin Group (NZ), 67 Apollo Drive, Rosedale, Auckland 0632, New Zealand
(a division of Pearson New Zealand Ltd.)
Penguin Books (South Africa) (Pty.) Ltd., 24 Sturdee Avenue, Rosebank, Johannesburg 2196,
South Africa
Penguin Books Ltd., Registered Offices: 80 Strand, London WC2R 0RL, England

While the author has made every effort to provide accurate telephone numbers and Internet addresses
at the time of publication, neither the publisher nor the author assumes any responsibility for errors or
for changes that occur after publication. Further, the publisher does not have any control over and
does not assume any responsibility for author or third-party websites or their content.

First edition: January 2012

Library of Congress Cataloging-in-Publication Data

Solin, Daniel R.
    The smartest money book you'll ever read : everything you need to know about growing, spending,
and enjoying your money / Daniel R. Solin.
        p.   cm.
    Includes bibliographical references and index.
    ISBN 978-0-399-53721-9
    1. Finance, Personal.   I. Title.
    HG179.S55237   2011
    332.024—dc23   2011035980

PRINTED IN THE UNITED STATES OF AMERICA

10 9 8 7 6 5 4 3 2 1

PUBLISHER'S NOTE: This publication is designed to provide accurate and authoritative information
in regard to the subject matter covered. It is sold with the understanding that the publisher is not engaged
in rendering legal, accounting, or other professional services. If you require legal advice or other expert
assistance, you should seek the services of a competent professional. Continued on page 277.

Most Perigee books are available at special quantity discounts for bulk purchases for sales promotions,
premiums, fund-raising, or educational use. Special books, or book excerpts, can also be created to fit
specific needs. For details, write: Special Markets, Penguin Group (USA) Inc., 375 Hudson Street, New
York, New York 10014.

To Millie and Jack.
With you as our future, I like our chances.

CONTENTS

PART FOUR
The Home Dilemma

PART FIVE
Rest Insured: Solving the Insurance Rubik's Cube

PART SIX
The Investment Industry: Friend and Foe

PART SEVEN
Don't Fight the Markets

PART EIGHT
Putting Your Money to Work

PART NINE
Real Retirement Planning

PART TEN
Life (and Death) Events

PART ELEVEN
Putting It All Together

PART TWELVE
Sources, Support, and Supplemental Reading

Reversal of Fortune

If the rules don't work, you change them.
—Alan Dershowitz, law professor and author

I t's sad that so few people achieve financial independence. Less than 3% of the U.S. population has $1.5 million or more in assets, free of debt, and this includes the equity in their homes. A recent study found that nearly half of Americans probably couldn't come up with $2,000 in 30 days. (If you're not familiar with terms like *assets* or *equity* or if you come across any other financial terms that you're not sure you know the meaning of, you will probably find them defined in the glossary.)

This reversal of fortune for so many Americans is dispiriting. This book will help put you on sound financial footing.

This is not a book about how to get rich quick. But even if you are 60 and broke, I can show you how to become free of financial worries in a year or so and then rebuild from there. If you have 5 to 10 years, I can show you how to become financially comfortable. If you have more time, or have a good starting base of assets, I can show you how to become wealthy.

You don't need a lot of money to implement my suggestions. You can start small. If you don't have a high income, if the value of your portfolio or your home has fallen, or if your retirement plans have been derailed, you can rebuild. The secret is to plan and budget.

If you're like most people, the lack of planning and budgeting is precisely the problem. It's boring. It's a hassle and it's time-consuming. Those problems can be solved with a few simple tools, many of which you'll find online. Obtaining information, making calculations, and making and tracking transactions are easy and even fun to do online. The power of the Internet lets you find, compare, and get the best deals available on financial services you are probably already using.

Harnessing the power of the Internet, along with solid goal setting, financial planning, budgeting, saving, and investing, will lead you to financial independence. I define "financial independence" as not working (unless you want to) and being able to live on interest, dividends, and reasonable withdrawals of capital.

You don't have to use the Internet to benefit from this book. The key things you'll be doing—setting financial goals, developing your approach to risk, allocating your investments, and deciding where to spend your money—are all things you can do with a pencil, paper, calculator, and telephone.

About the Internet and Mint.com

The problem with most financial planning tasks—and the main reason to use online tools—is that the amount of information to be gathered, massaged, and tracked can be massive.

If you're like most people, you buy hundreds of products and services from scores of sources every year. You probably also use many financial services, like life, health, disability, auto, and maybe business insurance, a few credit cards, a debit card, certainly a checking account and a savings account, certificates of deposit (CDs), a 401(k), and perhaps mutual funds, individual stocks, or bonds—and maybe some gold or other alternative investments.

That's where Mint.com comes in. Mint.com (www.mint.com) is the world's largest *free* online financial planning site. With more than 6 million registered users, Mint.com provides a range of useful and easy-to-use online budgeting, planning, tracking, and shopping tools that make controlling your finances as simple as clicking your mouse. Mint.com also provides links to approximately 16,000 banks, brokerage firms, mortgage companies, lenders, and other financial intermediaries. It puts you in the position of having them compete for your business.

I'll tell you more about Mint.com at points in the book where this site and its tools might benefit you. At those points, you'll see Mint.com's little mint-leaf logo and a bit about how the site can help you with that step or task or make that aspect of your financial life easier.

When you see the little mint-leaf logo, you can think of it like you would the little red chili peppers on the menu in an Asian restaurant that points out "hot and spicy" dishes. Use it or not at your discretion. You do not need to become a registered user of Mint.com to access the information referred to in the "Mint Hints" throughout this book.

I have no association with Mint.com, other than obtaining its agreement to use its logo in this book and to reference its website where appropriate.

Where We're Going

The investing principles in this book are grounded in the approach I presented in my four previous books on investing. You—not your advisers, planners, or bankers—are the one who is in charge of your financial life. Over the long term, you will not build wealth by what I call hyperactive investing or other attempts to chase outsized returns. But you will build wealth by investing in a portfolio of solid, diversified stock and bond index funds.

Don't hand responsibility for your financial future to a financial planner who may or may not have your best interests at heart. There are times you can benefit from having the right kind of financial planner, and I'll point those times out in this book.

My approach to financial planning—much like my approach to investing—will provide you with specific guidance for achieving your financial goals, in ways largely ignored by others. Here's what you can expect to learn:

1. How to rebuild from the devastating financial reversals of the past several years.

2. How to free up money to invest and begin the journey to put you on sound financial footing.

3. How to access the tools at Mint.com (if you choose to do so) for budgeting, tracking, investing, and shopping for financial services.

4. How to avoid becoming a victim of financial institutions who remain dedicated to making money at your expense.

5. Why financial planning is an absolute necessity in the current financial climate of turbulence and uncertainty.

I know this sounds like a tall order, but I think you'll be surprised at how easy it really is.

Let's get started.

PART ONE

Wrapping Your Mind Around Your Money

Building wealth—or reversing your downward spiral—takes thought and planning. That's because so many forces work hard to compel you to spend your money rather than save it. When you save money, equally powerful forces can operate to have your money work for you rather than for others. But you have to engage those positive forces.

In this part, you will start thinking about what you want from your money and how to go about achieving those goals.

CHAPTER 1

Bad Things Happen to Good People

Middle-class culture in the United States rests on the precepts of human capitalism—invest in your own skills and those of your children, and the market will reward you. These precepts now seem shakier than they have in the past.
—Nancy Folbre, economics professor, University of Massachusetts, Amherst

For more than 25 years, Paul Johnston owned and operated the Ever-Ready Copy Shop in Bergenfield, New Jersey. In 2001, the recession, and increasing competition from Kinko's and Staples, caused a sharp drop in business. In August 2002, Paul closed the shop. He began consulting with businesses in the electronics industry.

In January 2007, Paul was diagnosed with non-Hodgkin's lymphoma. After spending most of 2007 dealing with chemotherapy, he found a position as a technician with a microwave communications company. However, the company was acquired by a Dutch firm which laid off one-third of the workforce, including Paul. He quickly found work at a similar company, but when the 2008–2009 recession hit, Paul was laid off again.

In early 2008 Paul fell behind in his mortgage payments, and his lender began the process of foreclosing on his home. Before that time, he had paid all his bills and had decent credit.

Paul sought forbearance and loan modification. He was asked to fill out a detailed questionnaire and to include bank statements, pay stubs, tax returns, and hardship letters. Paul offered three formal modification proposals, none of which was acknowledged. He never spoke with anyone who could make a decision or even start to negotiate—at a time when banks and government agencies were saying they wanted to keep homeowners in their homes.

On March 15, 2010, Paul's home was put up for auction.

According to Paul, "[T]he auctioneer opened the bidding by taking an offer from the bank's representative for $447,000. This was far more than I had borrowed, and more than $100,000 over its most recent appraised value." There were no other bids. Several months later, Paul was evicted.

Paul Johnston is one of millions of people who have fallen out of the middle class and into perilous financial lives. As recently as 2010, soup kitchens strained to meet demand, serving formerly middle-class patrons for the first time. At one point in 2009, a record high *one in eight* Americans was receiving food stamps. Home foreclosures set new highs in 2010, with hundreds of thousands facing the loss of their dwellings. RealtyTrac, which reports on foreclosures, stated that in the first half of 2010, 1.6 million homes were in foreclosure. In March alone, 367,056 properties were the subject of foreclosure proceedings. Many borrowers took on loans they never should have, and some walked away from underwater mortgages. Others, like Paul, were caught in circumstances beyond their control, with no safety net.

When food and shelter become problems for millions of middle-class Americans, you know there's been a real shift in the economic landscape. Whether you are starting out in your career with worries about the job market or you are nearing retirement with a comfortable nest egg, this much is certain: Middle-class life isn't what it used to be. A key feature used to be predictability and a sense of financial security unknown to the poor. Middle-class people knew they had a roof over their heads, and it wasn't public shelter. They knew where their next meal was coming from, and it wasn't a soup kitchen. All that has changed.

I am not forecasting Armageddon or a market meltdown. I fully understand that America still offers tremendous economic opportunities. But whether you look at Washington or Wall Street, manufacturing or healthcare, retail or real estate, you will see increasing and increasingly complex problems. You will also notice a nearly complete absence of straight talk from policy makers about ways to solve these problems and reverse the decline of the middle class.

So, here's some straight talk.

It is up to each of us to take charge of our financial lives. We must take our decisions about income, purchases, savings, and investments seriously. Up to now, many of us have not. The average baby boomer (now 46 to 65 years of age) has well under $100,000 saved for retirement and faces a housing market that may be moribund for years to come. In the bubble-driven cheap-money booms of the 1990s and 2000s, many Americans lived beyond their means, incurred debts they couldn't repay, and took risks they couldn't handle. Many are now paying the price. I am not trying to blame anyone. My goal is to empower you to improve your financial situation, immediately and in the long term.

Let's start by examining the ways most of us make decisions

about money. The first rule of money management is inscribed below the home of the Oracle at Delphi in Greece: Know thyself.

What's the Point?

Effective money management is more important than ever.

CHAPTER 2

Lifestyles of the Broke and Homeless

I spent a lot of my money on booze, birds and fast cars.
The rest I just squandered.
—George Best, Irish soccer player

Building wealth is a skill you can learn. Yet many industries depend on your *not* learning to build wealth. The credit card industry, for example, aids and abets an entire system based on overspending, impulse buying, and shopping as sport or therapy.

In the years running up to the recession of 2008–2009, U.S. household consumer debt stood at an all-time high. In late 2008, there was nearly $1 trillion of credit card debt outstanding, up more than 25% since 2003. That was in addition to $10.5 trillion in mortgage debt.

Think of debt like a massive drain on your future income. While some debt, like a mortgage, may make sense (though you should carefully consider the terms and costs, covered in Part Four), consumer credit generally motivates you to spend more than you make. To build wealth, you must spend *less* than you make.

Compulsive shopping, casino gambling, day trading, and

borrowing to bet on market movements are extreme examples of bad debt behavior. The consequence of this activity is the high debt, low savings, and poor returns that plague most households and investors.

A Nation of Grasshoppers

The lessons of the Great Depression of the 1930s—that thrift and savings lead to financial security, if not guaranteed wealth— were lost after the 1970s. The table below shows the average U.S. saving rate (as a percent of gross national income) for the past five decades.

Decade	Net Saving as a Percent of Net National Income
1960s	9.9
1970s	8.6
1980s	5.7
1990s	4.8
2000s	2.3

From the 1960s through the 2000s, the national saving rate fell by more than 75%. Ironically, during that time, Americans developed a cultural fascination with "lifestyles of the rich and famous." It was a fascination with the amount of money spent to achieve those lifestyles rather than with building financial security.

As Charles Hugh Smith points out, "Americans are holding a fantasy-view of their piece of the American Dream/middle-class membership." He then adds, "Their 'membership' in the middle class is based on *perceived* membership gained by consumer activities such as shopping . . . the brand of car they drive . . . and other status symbols they feel reflect their 'values' and 'member-ship' in the middle class."

Meanwhile, during the 2000s, China's national saving rate ranged from *40% to 50%* of its GDP—dwarfing even the American rate of five decades ago. Moreover, the United States, with the world's largest economy—three times the size of China's—owes China $1 trillion. Americans have become spendthrift grasshoppers to China's industrious ants.

Americans are hard workers. They work more hours annually than any other workforce in the developed world. But Americans do not manage the fruits of their labor with anything approaching skill or even rationality.

Whether this arises from brain chemistry, shifting cultural values, or other forces I will leave to others to determine. The key issue here is, How can you begin to build wealth and secure your financial future?

I'll give you the answer right now: Place more value on *having* money than on spending it.

> ## mint hint
>
> You'll find features at Mint.com that visually portray the relationships between larger economic and financial developments and personal finance topics so they are easy to grasp. For an example, see "How the U.S. Credit Downgrade Could Hurt You" by John Ulzheimer (www.mint.com/blog/credit-2/how-us-credit-downgrade-could-hurt-you-082011).

What's the Point?

You work hard for your money. You have to work harder at keeping it.

CHAPTER 3

What Marshmallows Can Teach You About Money

The rich always think in terms of delayed gratification. . . .
This is the process they all have in common, whatever
they put their mind to.
—TheProbabilist.com

Nothing has more utility than money, especially in the long term.

Thanks to compounding, a dollar invested at an annual return of 10% will be worth $2.59 in 10 years, $6.73 in 20 years, and a whopping $17.45 in 30 years. This means if a 35-year-old invested $10,000 at an annual rate of return of 10% today, it will be worth almost $175,000 when she reaches the age of 65.

The time value of money is partly why nothing has more utility than money. But even in the present, cash in hand has unbeatable utility. That's why so many couples prefer gifts of money on their wedding day. Money clearly trumps soup tureens and popcorn poppers.

Still, many of us behave as if money had little utility, now or in the future. We make impulse purchases. We fail to budget, save, and invest. We even take on costly debt to buy things with far less utility than money.

To learn why, let's look at well-known research among school-children, conducted in the late 1960s and early 1970s. Stanford University psychology professor Walter Mischel's research aimed to test the ability of children to delay gratification—and what further implications it might hold. Mischel told each child that he or she could have one marshmallow now or two marsh-mallows in 15 minutes. The child could ring a bell to call the researcher into the room if he or she couldn't hold out. (Some kids just grabbed the treat when the researcher left the room.)

In follow-up interviews years later, Mischel found that the high delayers, those who held out for the two marshmallows, were more likely to have higher SAT scores (on average 210 points higher!). They were also less likely to have behavioral problems and were more likely to maintain friendships. Mischel and his colleagues tracked the subjects into their late 30s and found that the low delayers were more likely to have drug problems and had significantly higher body mass indexes. Mischel views de-layed gratification as a key to success. "If you can deal with [strong immediate desires], then you can study for the SAT in-stead of watching television. And you can save money for retire-ment. It's not just about marshmallows."

That's because one of the most critical factors in wealth build-ing is time. Money will work for you if you put it to work, and the longer it works for you, the more wealth you will build. The time factor has two major implications. One is the well-known magic (actually, the mathematics) of compound interest. But time is important for another, less widely understood, reason.

The longer your investment horizon, the better you can deal with risk. A longer time horizon lets you weather the inevitable but unpredictable ups and downs of the market. It also reduces the chance that you'll need to withdraw your money at a time when your assets have declined in value.

mint hint

Mint.com provides a huge array of tools and resources to assist you in managing every key aspect of your finances. For a quick introduction, see the video "90-Second Overview: The Best Free Way to Manage Your Money" (www.youtube .com/watch?v=rK6WLHNYjwM).

What value do you place on money? Answer each of the following questions with very high, high, low, or very low:

- What, to you, is the value of having money work for you?

- What, to you, is the value of staying out of debt?

- What is the value to you of having savings to get you through periods of unemployment or other financial setbacks?

- What value do you place on being able to retire comfortably or to cut back your working hours down the road?

- What value do you place on being able to handle investment risk with no loss of sleep?

If you value each of these things as "high" or "very high," you are ready to start setting some financial goals.

What's the Point?

Decide for yourself what value you place on money, then plan and act accordingly.

CHAPTER 4

A Map Won't Help Without a Destination

Every day I get up and look through the *Forbes* list of the richest
people in America. If I'm not there, I go to work.

—Robert Orben, author and speechwriter

In the 1950s, TV shows like *The Millionaire* and movies like *How
to Marry a Millionaire* were popular. Back then, most people considered being a millionaire the pinnacle of financial success
and security. Since then, we've seen decades of inflation, but the
goal of becoming a millionaire is still compelling to most of us.

Is it enough?

Let's say you have no debt, you own your home free and clear,
and you have $1 million invested at only a 5% annual return.
That will produce an annual income of $50,000—equal to the
2009 median U.S. family income, according to the Census
Bureau.

Even after taxes, you can live well in most regions of the
United States on $50,000, if you have no mortgage and no debt.
You may, however, want to set your long-term financial goals
even higher.

Financial goals help you allocate your income to the things

you value most. They help you get the most satisfaction, fun, and security for your money.

When you set goals and save for major purchases like a house or car, you minimize the debt you have to take on to buy them.

Targeting certain amounts by certain dates for certain purposes lets you measure your progress. It helps you get back on track or set new goals if your circumstances change. Finally, goals you care about motivate you to make a budget and stay on track.

Set Short- and Long-Term Goals

To set useful goals you have to address both short-term and long-term financial needs and contingencies. If you set only a large, long-term goal, such as retiring with $1 million in 25 years, you may sacrifice many things that would have made you happier in the meantime, and even hurt yourself financially. For example, if you put every spare cent into an IRA, you might have to access that account and incur penalties if you need those funds in an emergency. Yet, putting all your money into short-term accounts isn't the answer either, because money invested for longer periods generally earns a higher return.

Think of short-term goals as those you can achieve within five years, and long-term goals as those that will take more than five years.

One useful short-term goal is to get out of debt. If you are carrying high-interest debt, consider the goal of getting out of it in two or three years. The rate on most credit cards and loans is so high that you can often earn a better return on your money by first paying off your debt and then starting a serious saving and investing plan. (There are exceptions, so read Part Three before you start paying down debt.)

If you want to retire in 20 years instead of 30, if you want a home in a certain community, or if you want to spend a year in a foreign country, then write those down as goals.

The key is to have *motivating* goals. Getting out of debt may or may not be motivating to you. If it's not, frame that goal in terms you do find motivating, such as taking an annual vacation with the interest you used to give to creditors.

You may be tempted to put off longer-term goal setting. Don't. Setting a goal of becoming independently wealthy and saving even small amounts toward that goal will help you develop the ongoing focus that's necessary to achieving it.

> ### mint hint
>
> Mint.com's "Goals" feature lets you set different goals and tie them to your budget. It walks you through setting and achieving each goal and helps you determine how much money you'll need, define an achievable first step, and develop realistic expectations of how long it will take.
>
> See "How to Set and Track Financial Goals with Mint" by Rob Griffiths (www.mint.com/blog/goals/how-to-use-mints-goals-06302010).

What's the Point?

Setting specific, actionable, motivating goals will turbocharge your wealth-building efforts.

PART TWO

Master Your Universe

Decide what kind of future you want to live in. Financial planning is making those decisions, translating them into goals, and creating a plan that moves you toward those goals.

CHAPTER 5

Focus on Your Net Worth

Net worth equals the sum of assets attributable to any individual
15 years and older in a household less any liabilities. . . .
Assets matter for all families for both economic
security and social mobility.
—2009–2010 Assets and Opportunity Scorecard Corporation
for Enterprise Development (CFED)

Net worth is the number you want to maximize. Net worth is
your assets (your money and property) minus your liabilities (your debts).

Don't borrow to improve your lifestyle. When you borrow,
you focus on earning enough to service the debt. Lenders ask
about your income but never about your net worth. They don't
want you thinking about your net worth, because borrowing
reduces it.

A typical balance sheet shows assets, liabilities, and net worth
at a certain date. Assets are listed on the left. Liabilities and net
worth are listed to the right. The formula for net worth is: Assets −
Liabilities = Net Worth. When the U.S. Census Bureau looks at net
worth, they use "household balance sheets" and this formula.

I'm going to show you how to draw up a rough balance sheet
for your household.

Assets include cash in all bank accounts, certificates of deposit (CDs), stocks and bonds, money market funds, mutual funds, savings bonds, Treasury securities, Individual Retirement Accounts (IRAs), 401(k)s, and other retirement accounts. Assets also include property, such as your house(s), car(s), furniture, and any valuables. But we're concerned mainly with cash and investments that could be converted to cash. If you own your home, value it at the recent sales price of comparative homes in your neighborhood. You don't need a formal appraisal.

Your liabilities are your debts. Use the total amounts due from your most recent statements and the total amount outstanding on your mortgage.

The balance sheet here uses round numbers and typical accounts for a household. Normally, a balance sheet (a financial statement that accountants and businesses use) lists assets on the left and both liabilities and net worth together on the right. Total Assets must equal Total Liabilities and Net Worth. (The two sides must balance.)

SAMPLE BALANCE SHEET ACCOUNTS FOR A FAMILY

	Assets		Liabilities	Net Worth
Cash: checking account	$7,000	Credit Card #1	$12,000	
Cash: savings account	$2,000	Credit Card #2	$5,000	
1-year CD	$8,000	Credit Card #3	$3,000	
Stock in ABC Company	$10,000	Car loan (sedan)	$15,000	
Car: sedan (late model)	$20,000	Mortgage	$275,000	
Car: minivan (older)	$5,000	Home equity loan	$40,000	
Boat (22-foot sailboat)	$8,000			
Home	$325,000			
IRA	$70,000			
Total	**$455,000**		**$350,000**	**$105,000**

The table on the opposite page presents balance sheet accounts for a typical family. The major account groups—assets, liabilities, and net worth—are arranged to reflect the formula for net worth. It demonstrates that you will maximize your net worth by maximizing your assets and minimizing your liabilities.

Calculating your net worth is motivating because when you examine your own balance sheet accounts, a few things become clear.

First, debt is the enemy of your wealth. You can have $3 million in assets, but if you have $4 million in debt, your net worth is *minus* $1 million. You have no wealth.

Second, there are liquid assets and there are noncash assets. Many noncash assets *cost* money to own, operate, maintain, and insure.

Third, your home may or may not be a great investment. If you have paid off the mortgage *and* you can sell it for a price that reflects its value *and* the property taxes are reasonable, then it may be a great investment. If not, it may be a drag on your finances.

On paper, the family represented by the sample balance sheet account has the problems that many U.S. households face. They live in a heavily mortgaged home. They have a lot of debt and little invested. (Their ages, marital status, and family size are not relevant because I'm just showing how to use the balance sheet.) Although

> ### mint hint
>
> Tracking your net worth is essential, but it's tedious. Mint.com can put your net worth calculations on automatic pilot.
>
> After you are set up (which takes about five minutes) Mint.com links to your checking, savings, credit card, and investment accounts. It pulls the information together for you and makes it easy to see your assets, liabilities, and net worth.
>
> To sign up for Mint.com, visit www.mint.com or go directly to the secure sign-up page (https://wwws.mint.com/login.event).

they're better off than many families, they are a long way from a net worth that would classify them as wealthy.

What's the Point?

Your focus should be on increasing your net worth.

CHAPTER 6

The Thrill of a Budget Beats the Agony of Poverty

A billion here, a billion there—sooner or later it adds
up to real money.
—Everett Dirksen, U.S. senator

The word *budgeting* makes many people cringe. A budget is just a way of making decisions about your money consciously instead of unconsciously. With a budget, you make better decisions.

You're on a budget whether you know it or not. Pretending you're not on a budget leads to overspending on things you can't afford. That undermines your goal of creating wealth by increasing your net worth.

In budgeting you decide how to allocate your monthly income to your monthly expenses, what those expenses will be, and how much you will save each month.

Drawing up a budget starts with gathering information about your income and spending. These numbers come from your savings and checking account deposits and withdrawals (at ATMs and via debit card), your checkbook, your credit card statements, and, if you have them, receipts for cash expenditures.

The more you detail your expenses, the better. Definitely account for your major expenses, and all recurrent minor ones. Strive to identify *at least* 95% of your spending.

Personal finance writer Ramit Sethi notes that many people waste 20% to 30% of their money without knowing where it goes. That happens when you have payments, like auto, health, or life insurance premiums or fees, deducted from your bank account without checking on increases or totaling the annual amounts. These payments can skyrocket if you don't monitor them and occasionally shop for better deals.

Untracked cash or credit card purchases also add up. The usual suspects include online shopping, take-out meals, evenings in bars and restaurants, and daily lattes and gourmet muffins.

A Sample Budget

A budget lists your monthly income and expenses. A budget should start with your current income and expenses so you know where your money came from and where it went to. Then you can identify areas where you can reduce your spending and maybe areas where you should be allocating more money, usually to savings and perhaps insurance or home or auto maintenance.

The table on the next page shows ideal budgets for three different types of households.

These percentages are pre-tax. If they seem too low to you, it may be that you are thinking about them as after-tax.

With these sample budgets, if you are debt free or close to it, money that would have gone to debt payments can go to savings or other uses. The "mystery cash" category accounts for the small amount of money that you just can't seem to track no matter how

SUGGESTED SPENDING (AS PERCENTAGES OF GROSS INCOME)

Annual Expenses	Single (%)	Married (%)	Parents (%)
Housing, utilities	20–23	23–25	22–25
Taxes	17–19	18–20	19–21
Savings, investments	8–9	8–10	7–8
Food	8–9	8–9	8–9
Debt payments	8–9	4–5	1–2
Vacation, entertainment, hobbies	7–9	7–8	5
Insurance	2–4	2–5	4–6
Car, gasoline, transportation	7–8	6–7	4–5
Clothing, personal care	4	4–5	5–6
Gifts, contributions	3–4	5–7	5–6
Medical expenses	1–2	2–3	2–3
Child care, education	1–2	1	7–8
Unreimbursed business expenses	1–2	1–2	1–2
Mystery cash (rounding errors)	1	1	1

hard you try. Since each situation is different, you should include any other category of expenses that is applicable.

This budget calls for saving 7% to 10% of your gross (pre-tax) income.

Build a Budget

Get hold of your income and spending records for 6 months or preferably 12. Your goal is to develop a monthly budget, but some expenses are not monthly. Payments for auto insurance and repairs, healthcare and dental expenses, home repairs, and

mint hint

Mint makes budgeting much easier than tracking your spending in each category (restaurants, rent, insurance, etc.) by hand. By linking your credit or debit card, Mint will automatically pull in your new purchases each night, categorize them, and check them against your budget category to see if you've gone over. If you have, you can get an alert through email, text message, or using the Mint iPhone or Android app.

Also, with more than 6 million members, Mint.com shows you what the average household spends on a particular category when you are setting up your budget. For example, the average household spends about $30 each month on coffee shops. If you want to challenge yourself to cut back, use that figure for a little competition.

seasonal outlays often occur irregularly. For those expenses, divide the annual totals by 12 (or 6-month totals by 6) to get the monthly amounts.

When you first draw up your budget, use the sample budget categories or create your own. The key is to see where your money is going and how you stack up against the ideal allocations. After you've done that, you can improve your financial situation by reducing and reallocating your expenses. That's the planning part of bud-geting.

When you draw up a new budget that reflects your goals, don't expect to reach the new levels in a few weeks. It may take months, or even a year or two. However long it takes, it's worth it to get your finances under control and to save and invest for your future.

What's the Point?

Your money comes in and goes out whether or not you track it. Budgeting is the first step toward getting control of your finances and increasing your net worth.

CHAPTER 7

Pay Yourself First

Putting money away systematically is the best way to "dollar cost average" and save for retirement.
—Jim Lentini, president, Lentini Insurance & Investments Inc.

Banks have various ways of attracting depositors, and some are more useful than others. Among the most attractive are automatic savings plans, which virtually any bank will set up for you. The bank will transfer specific amounts from checking to savings on specific days of the month. This is the surest way to save money.

Initially target your savings *at least* 5% of your income and increase that to 20% (or more) as quickly as possible. The exception would be if you have debt with high interest. Getting that off your balance sheet would probably be the best first step.

Otherwise, pay yourself first. An automatic savings plan keeps money out of your hands. It takes your savings off the top of your income, just like the IRS takes taxes.

Most employers offer direct deposit of payroll checks. This makes having a specific amount transferred to savings on payday a snap. Many employers also offer automatic retirement savings plans, typically a 401(k). Automatic savings, particularly for retirement, is a great idea—especially if there is an employer match. Make the minimum contribution necessary to maximize the employer contribution. Otherwise, you are passing up free money.

To meet the goals you set in Part One, set up a separate interest-bearing account. You also need an account for emergency or periodic expenses like dental care, car repairs, and replacement of appliances.

Ensuring that the money is there when the transfer is made can require more focus if you're self-employed and don't receive regular, reliable paychecks. In that case, just as you pay quarterly estimated income taxes, you have to plan your cash flow to fund the automatic transfer to savings on specified dates. (You also need automatic transfers into an income tax savings account.)

Whether you are employed or self-employed, the key to a successful automatic savings plan is to start with an amount you know you can cover and then periodically increase that amount. Start small (even if it's under 5%) and increase the amount as you develop the saving habit.

Boost Your Automatic Savings

Here are a two more tips about automatic savings plans:

- **Know the interest rate you are earning and shop interest rates periodically.** Rates fluctuate and if you can earn higher interest for a similar term, you should. Beware of CDs that lock up your money for long terms. Money market accounts pay rates competitive with savings accounts, but without long terms. At first, the amounts you earn by shopping rates may seem small, but they add up. Also, you will develop the habit of monitoring how hard your money is (or isn't) working for you.

- **Keep savings and checking accounts in separate banks.** You will generally find higher interest rates by shopping. Having your accounts at separate banks discourages you from dipping into savings. Avoid banks that charge fees (and particularly high fees) for fund transfers or checking services, if possible.

mint hint

Mint.com automatically checks your current interest rates against the latest offers from major financial institutions. Rather than watching interest rates each day, Mint has a "Ways to Save" tab that shows you how much money you would save if you refinanced your mortgage or switched to a different credit card or savings account. You can also browse through hundreds of financial products using filters like no-fee checking or cash-back credit card rewards.

What's the Point?

Automatic savings plans can help you achieve your goals.

CHAPTER 8

Build Savings Muscle

Money is a limited resource, whether it is a government, a business, or even a household. Wise budget planning, along with a desire to live within this boundary, is key to managing this resource.
—Ashton McDonald, college student, Missouri

In his bestseller *The Abs Diet*, Dave Zinczenko notes that simply due to basic resting metabolism "between 60 and 80 percent of your daily calories are burned up doing nothing." Digesting your food burns between 10% and 30% of your daily calories. Exercise and movement burn only 10% to 15%. You also burn calories just by breathing and sleeping.

Zinczenko recommends exercises that increase metabolism and create muscle, which raises your basic metabolic rate. That way, you're burning more calories on autopilot.

Most of your money goes out the door on autopilot. Monthly expenses like mortgage, cable, phone, and insurance premiums burn most of your income. Emergency expenses and untracked out-of-pocket spending accounts for most of the rest.

Think of monthly expenses as your monetary metabolism—the rate at which you're burning your money. You want to burn fewer dollars.

If you own a car, consider its effect on your monetary metabolism. Are the monthly loan or lease payments high? How about the insurance premiums? Do you have frequent expensive repairs? Lower your monetary metabolism by trading your car in for one that burns fewer dollars.

Subject your rent or mortgage (see Part Four) and all insurance premiums (see Part Five) to similar scrutiny.

Study your food and entertainment budget. Try to view eating out and socializing at bars as expensive bad habits that should be reserved for special occasions.

Constantly ask yourself, How can I free up more money for savings and investment?

How to Cut Spending Fast

First, firmly commit to your goals and to changing your behavior to reach them, and then pick a cost-cutting method you will actually use.

If you are in negative cash flow, crushing debt (see Part Three), or nearing insolvency, you'll need to adopt a "financial siege" mentality. This means minimizing every single expense. Many people (and companies) go bankrupt because they don't adjust quickly to major financial setbacks or mistakes. Hope is not a plan. Sell your car and ride the bus or a bike. Eliminate *every* nonessential expense, such as cable TV, health clubs, and coffee-of-the-month clubs.

Consider moving to a cheaper area of the country. Tens of thousands of residents have fled Long Island for upstate New York, California for Arizona, and the Northeast for the Midwest or South. Benefits include less expensive housing and, often, lower-cost lifestyles and social expectations.

If you are in basically good financial shape but need to increase your savings, focus first on a few areas where you can free up money fairly painlessly. The usual suspects include frequent stops at cafés or bars, online shopping and mall crawling, high-end hairdressers and barbers, and your favorite (over)indulgence, whether it's cosmetics, clothing, or cheese. Also, can you really afford that expensive vacation every year?

You'll achieve the greatest savings by controlling *both* monthly expenses and out-of-pocket spending. Out-of-pocket spending is often unconscious. Control it and you will lower your monetary metabolic burn rate.

While many advisers say pay in cash, there are costs to doing that. Trips to the ATM add up, and cash spending is difficult and time-consuming to track. Better to use your *no-transaction-fee* credit or debit card for all purchases and track whether you are on, over, or under budget.

🌿 mint hint

Simply reviewing all of your household spending will help you identify where you can cut back. Mint offers iPhone, Android, and iPad applications, which allow you to check up on your latest purchases, your current balances across all your bank accounts (whether your bank offers a mobile app or not), and see how you're doing on your budget—*before* you spend. They'll even send you updates when you're over budget. It's a good way to pass time when you're in line at the grocery store—and more profitable than playing games or checking email.

No one system works for everyone. If paying cash works for you, pay cash. If cards work for you, use cards. Just know where your money is going and what you are getting in return. Keep your goals in mind at all times. Change your thinking—and spending—so you save systematically.

The feeling that you are moving toward financial freedom will be more than worth the effort.

What's the Point?

Drop your monthly expenses well below your monthly take-home pay and you'll free up thousands of dollars a year for savings and investment.

PART THREE

Freedom from Debt

Debt in all its forms undermines your financial future. Debt diverts money from savings and investing *and* from future spending. The interest is often exorbitant and can exponentially increase the price of your purchase.

There are wise uses of debt, but they are very few. In this part, you'll learn how to use debt wisely, minimize the costs of credit, and get out of debt if you are in over your head.

CHAPTER 9

Don't Abet Debt

A man in debt is so far a slave.
—Ralph Waldo Emerson, American poet and philosopher

The 2000s economic boom was fueled largely by debt. Toward the end of that expansion, consumer borrowings stood at record highs.

"Consumers' outlays have outpaced the growth of their income for a long time," *Business Week* noted in late 2007. "Lenders learned how to judge risk and expand the pool of potential borrowers—and the party was on. 'The most important factor has been that it is easier to borrow,' says Christopher D. Carroll, a Johns Hopkins University economist."

Just because it is easy to borrow doesn't mean you should.

The two key things to understand are (1) every time you borrow money you erode your future income, and (2) when you borrow you *immediately* reduce your net worth, except when you use the loan to buy something of equal or greater value.

It's unwise to pay for restaurant meals, vacations, and other expenses with a credit card unless you pay the full balance every month. It can make sense to borrow to buy a house. But the term of the loan should match (or be shorter than) the life of the asset being financed.

That's the way businesses generally use credit. They use long-term loans to buy long-term assets, like productive equipment, and short-term loans to fund short-term assets, like inventories.

What about student loans? In theory, they are okay because you will have your education for the rest of your life, and education increases earnings. In practice, you might be paying off student loans for what seems like the rest of your life. From a financial perspective, a student loan is best used to pay for studies that produce enough income to pay off the loan.

Shop aggressively for the best rate, fees, and terms. The rate is the effective annual rate you pay on the loan. Always calculate the cost of what you are purchasing, the amount you are borrowing, and the *total amount* you will have to repay. That last figure can be a real eye-opener (as you'll see in Part Four, which covers mortgages).

Fees are part of the total cost of borrowing. When you compare loan costs, add fees to the total amount you must pay. Be especially aware of application and origination fees, prepayment penalties, and late payment fees. The latter are notoriously high on credit cards.

If you have a good credit history and credit score (see Chapter 12), you can ask prospective lenders to waive fees and try to negotiate a better rate or terms. Shop to find the best deal, and ask other lenders to beat it. Service representatives (or their supervisors) often have the power to give an applicant with good credit a better deal *but you have to ask*.

Managing Your Debt

The best way to manage debt is to avoid it or eliminate it. Use credit cards only when you pay the balances every month *and* when there is an interest-free "grace period" on purchases. Avoid cash advances on credit cards. They carry very high annual rates and have no grace periods.

Never cosign a loan unless you can afford (and want) to make the payments if the borrower defaults. Many people—usually parents—cosign loans only to get stuck with the payments.

Never borrow to speculate in the financial markets. Brokers encourage "margin trading" to generate interest income for their firms. You wouldn't borrow to gamble in a casino, so don't do it in the markets. People who dabble in house flipping, stock options, or commodities trading after taking a course or reading a book almost always lose money. When they are using borrowed money, they wind up in deep financial trouble.

If you are self-employed, make your estimated federal and state income tax payments on time. If you don't, you may have to borrow to pay your taxes, which is preferable to paying late because the penalties and interest charged by the IRS make rates charged by consumer lenders appear reasonable.

mint hint

Mint.com enables you to compare credit card offers based on introductory rates, annual rates, cash back or miles, and the amount you'll save over one, two, or three years given your typical balances. Mint.com also lets you screen card offers based on the types and percentage of spending you do on your credit card in categories like air travel, restaurants, and office supplies.

For an excellent introduction to credit cards, see the video "Choosing a Credit Card" at Mint.com (https://www.mint.com/credit/choosing-a-credit-card).

If you are in debt, track your payments, interest, fees, and total debt every month. Loan payments and minimum monthly payments on credit cards are designed to keep you in debt for years. Seeing how your debt adds up will motivate you to reduce or eliminate it.

I strongly recommend zero debt, except for a mortgage, which you should prepay to the extent that you can afford. (See Part Four.) If you are spending more than 5% of your income on non-mortgage debt, consider more aggressive repayment. Commit to get out of debt and then do it quickly.

What's the Point?

Avoid debt, but if you do use credit, use it to finance only assets of equal or greater value. Shop rates and terms, and repay loans as quickly as possible.

CHAPTER 10

Debt Out!

Debt is the worst poverty.
—Thomas Fuller, English preacher and historian

Poverty caused by excessive debt can hit suddenly, when you face a major expense or lose your job. Or it can build slowly as month after month you see your money increasingly going to creditors. Many people find both forces at work.

Until mid-2008, Philadelphia-area resident Diane "was a dream customer for lenders," according to the *New York Times*. She carried two adjustable-rate mortgages, an auto loan, and credit card debt—with interest payments and fees that totaled more than 40% of her pre-tax income of $48,000.

Diane was handling the more than $20,000 in annual interest payments that major financial institutions were charging her, until medical emergencies and job loss "pushed her over the edge." Her home went into foreclosure and her financial life was in ruin.

When you avoid debt, you avoid the poverty it can generate. But what if you are already carrying high consumer debt?

If you want to build wealth, you must get out of debt.

Most U.S. middle-income families see credit as essential to their financial lives. Most have no idea how much it costs them and how it undermines their financial future.

To motivate yourself to get out of debt, find out what it costs you, and then develop a plan. If you prepared a budget and calculated your net worth in Part Two, you know what you're paying to creditors each month and how much your debt has reduced your net worth. You also know how much you can afford to save each month.

Here's how to develop a plan for getting out of debt.

Steps to Freedom from Debt

First, getting out of debt can be as hard as any diet or exercise program. Abandon the idea that you will win the lottery and pay off your debts. Stop buying whatever you want when you want it. The psychological reasons for debt can be hard to address. Go back to your goals from Part One, recommit to them, and realize that debt breeds poverty.

Second, if you're in a hole, stop digging. Cut up your credit cards. Save one for car rentals, hotel reservations, and online purchases, when you can afford these things again. If car payments are a problem, sell your car, pay off the loan, and get a cheaper car. Your mortgage is the only acceptable debt.

Third, total up your loan and card balances and monthly payments. Learn how much of each payment is applied to interest and principal, and what you are paying in interest and fees. Identify which loans and cards are costing you the most interest and fees.

Fourth, put as much of your credit card debt as possible on the lowest-cost credit card you can find. Cards with low introductory rates on balance transfers are still available, if you have good credit and are current on all payments. Move high-interest balances to that card and pay it off before the higher rate kicks in. Minimize the number of times you do this, because it may affect your credit rating.

Fifth, use the money you budgeted for saving in Part Two to pay more than the monthly minimum on the highest-cost loan or credit card until it's paid off. Do this until you have paid off all of your borrowings.

You might also consider tapping *low-cost* sources of funds. If you own your home, a home equity loan *could* be the answer. It can provide lower interest over the life of the loan, and you can deduct the interest from your income for tax purposes. Even if it takes five to seven years, the end will be in sight—because you're taking on *no new debt*, which is essential to successful loan consolidation with a home equity loan.

As a last-ditch maneuver you may be able to borrow against your 401(k) or an IRA at a low rate. But *do not* withdraw money from a tax-advantaged retirement account to pay off debt.

Finally, if you have debt you just can't handle, take stronger action (see Chapter 11).

> ### 🌿 mint hint
>
> Under the "Goals" section on Mint, try the "Pay Off Credit Card Debt" goal. You can use slider bars to adjust how much you can afford to put toward paying down your debt, and Mint will calculate how long it will be before you're debt free, and how much interest you'll pay along the way. It's eye-opening. The end result is a month-by-month guide to which card to pay off first and how much to pay on each card every month until you are debt free. And with Mint's bill reminder service, you will be notified prior to your credit card payment being due, thus avoiding costly late payment fees and extra finance charges.

Clean Up and Stay Clean

Once you join the ranks of the debt free, you'll find yourself able to save and invest. You'll see the asset side of your balance sheet grow, the liabilities side shrink, and your net worth increase.

It's a wonderful feeling of freedom, responsibility, and prosperity—it can be even more addictive than shopping!

What's the Point?

Picture your debt as a target. Take aim at it every day.

CHAPTER 11

The Nuclear Debt Option

The steady climb of consumer filings notwithstanding the
2005 bankruptcy law restrictions demonstrate that families
continue to turn to bankruptcy as a result of high debt
burdens and stagnant income growth.
—Samuel J. Gerdano, executive director,
American Bankruptcy Institute

Are you hopelessly in debt?

You have to take aggressive steps. The best option is to settle or restructure the debt with your creditors. Use a credit counselor if you need one. If you are in too much debt for those options to work, then declaring bankruptcy is the remaining option.

Settling or restructuring debt affects your credit history and scores. Once your debt is settled, you can rebuild your credit in 2 to 3 years. Declaring bankruptcy remains on your credit record for 10 years. Employers, landlords, and business associates take a dim view of poor credit histories.

If debt settlement or restructuring—or bankruptcy—is your only option, take steps quickly. Acting fast keeps you from incurring more debt, and can help you recover sooner.

Dealing with Creditors—or Credit Counselors

You don't need a credit counselor, but it can help. If you feel you can deal directly with your creditors, here's how to go about it.

Creditors are just people trying to do their jobs. Be professional. Have your records and budget in order and know the terms of your mortgage, loans, and credit cards and what you have paid on them.

Decide whether you want to restructure the debt or offer to settle for a lesser sum. Restructuring means making the loan more affordable by stretching out the repayment over time, lowering the interest, or eliminating fees. Settlement is paying less than the full sum you owe and having the debt wiped out. The lender will report the amount of debt forgiven as income to the IRS, and you will have to pay taxes on it.

Deal only with a representative who can make decisions. They will usually be in the remediation department. Be businesslike, but try to establish a relationship with them. If possible, meet in person.

You can involve a credit counselor in the negotiations. Visit the website of the National Foundation for Credit Counseling (www.nfcc.org) for names and locations of reputable credit counselors near you. There are *many* unscrupulous people calling themselves credit counselors. They make their money by charging fees to debtors and delivering little to no service. In contrast, legitimate credit counselors are paid by the banks, credit card companies, and other creditors (who are interested in getting something rather than nothing from distressed creditors).

Use a credit counselor if you find financial matters confusing or you can't negotiate with creditors. A good counselor will help you understand your situation and even deal with creditors for you. Credit counselors usually aim to get troubled borrowers onto a debt management plan.

Debt Management Plans

In a debt management plan you make monthly payments to a credit counseling agency, which then pays your creditors. If you work with an NFCC member agency, 100% of your payments go to your creditors.

A debt management plan is worked out by the credit counseling agency. They work regularly with creditors and know how the plans work. They can also obtain reduced or forgiven fees and help you reestablish your credit when you've repaid your debts.

Obtaining credit counseling will not show up on your credit report. But if you reach a settlement with one or more creditors or go onto a debt management plan, it will be disclosed. Payments you make on time under the new arrangement will be reported as current.

It usually takes three to five years to become debt free under a debt management plan, but people who go through the process can usually rebuild their credit fairly quickly.

Declaring Bankruptcy

Don't even consider bankruptcy without credit and legal advice. The lawyer you select should specialize in bankruptcy matters. Bankruptcy is a court-supervised method of having certain debts wiped out due to inability to pay. Legislation passed in 2005 favored creditors (who lobbied hard for its passage). Bankruptcy is not the totally fresh start it once was. Some credit card debts and most student loans are no longer discharged under the new law.

The new law mandates credit counseling before declaring bankruptcy. Consult a competent nonprofit credit counselor before consulting an attorney.

If you do declare bankruptcy you won't be alone. In 2010, 1.5 million U.S. consumers filed for bankruptcy, up from 1.4 million in 2009. In fact, in the five years following the 2005 bankruptcy legislation (2006–2010), more than *5 million* U.S. consumers declared bankruptcy.

This figure represents only people who reached the end of their borrowing rope. A multiple of that number continued under the stress of high debt. If that includes you, address the problem now.

> ### mint hint
>
> For a humorous but serious animated story about how to avoid the kind of trouble that credit cards can lead to, view the Mint.com mini-epic "Quest for Credit" (www.mint.com/blog/goals/quest -for-credit-complete-version).

What's the Point?

If you see no way to pay off your nonmortgage debt in three to five years, schedule a session with a qualified credit counselor.

CHAPTER 12

Edit Your Credit

For the first time since the installation of the FICO scoring
system in 1989, 35% of the population is now scoring below 650.
This is up from 27%, which was largely unchanged for
much of the past two decades.
—John Ulzheimer, president of consumer education,
SmartCredit.com

Why do you need a good credit score? Potential employers, business partners, and landlords expect people to have good credit. Good credit signals a person's ability to manage their financial affairs.

Your credit history is primarily the payment record for your loans, mortgage, and credit card debt. A credit report shows your identifying information (name, Social Security number, etc.) and the following:

- **Account information:** Date opened, date closed, balances, and payment history on mortgages, credit cards, and auto, student, and other loans (savings and checking accounts are usually not reported). Any late payment can affect your score.

- **Credit inquiries:** Parties who accessed your credit report in the past two years.

- **Other items:** Foreclosures, suits, judgments (satisfied or not), liens, bankruptcies, and accounts referred to collection agencies.

To handle their volume of credit decisions, many lenders rely on credit scoring. Some do their own scoring in-house based on the potential borrower's credit history, years of employment, years in his or her home, and other factors. Some rely completely on credit scores from credit agencies, and some use a credit score as part of their own system.

The FICO score, calculated by the Fair Isaac Corporation, is the most widely used score in the United States. FICO scores range from 300 to 850 and consider payment record, loan balances, number of accounts, age of accounts, collection accounts, bankruptcies, and other factors. A score of 750 or higher is generally considered good. Also, according to credit expert John Ulzheimer, "in today's financial services environment many lenders and insurance companies consider the ±650 point to be the dividing line between prime and sub-prime."

Prospective lenders use credit scores to measure creditworthiness because they have found that the scores distinguish good from bad credit risks and help predict loan losses.

Steps Toward Creditworthiness

How can you rebuild your credit if you have fallen behind in your bills, had your car repossessed, undergone foreclosure, or declared bankruptcy?

There are several steps that you can take.

First, realize there is no way to game the system. Credit data are supplied to and gathered by the credit reporting agencies in reasonably reliable, computerized ways. Credit scores are calculated on that data.

Second, get current on your bills and stay current. Use the debt reduction program in Chapter 10. Remain current on all loans and pay more than the minimum on the costliest one. Never let an account go past due unless you must, and then get current as quickly as possible.

Third, be consistent and diligent. It takes two to three years to rebuild your credit.

Fourth, use only the credit you need. Don't take multiple loans and cards to raise your creditworthiness. This can hurt your credit score because you can increase your lenders' exposure—and lower your score—with unused lines of credit. Also, you will lower your average account age. A higher average account age is better for your score.

Fifth, if you shop rates, do it within a 30-day period before you accept the mortgage, loan, or credit card. When you shop rates, each lender you approach registers a credit inquiry. These show up on your credit report and in your score. (If you check your own credit report, it doesn't count as an inquiry.)

As noted in Chapters 10 and 11, if you need credit counseling, get it. Don't exacerbate the harm to your creditworthiness by floundering in debt you can't handle.

Watch Out!

When you use the debt reduction program in Chapter 10, don't move balances too often or you will lower your credit score. The goal of that program is to lower your interest and fees *and* to pay the debt down faster, not to move balances around. Closing a

mint hint

For an insider look at credit and the credit industry, see John Ulzheimer's blog at Mint.com (for example, www.mint.com/blog/updates/your-credit-questions-answered-video-qa-with-expert-john-ulzheimer). John is the credit blogger for Mint.com and president of consumer education at Smart Credit.com, another excellent resource for information about credit.

credit card or paying off a loan doesn't remove it from your credit history. It will be reflected as a closed account.

Finally, you are viewed by lenders as more creditworthy if you have used loans and credit cards and handled them responsibly than if you have never used credit. So, if you are young and starting out, have a credit card and use mortgage or student loans if you need them, but only if you can pay them off as agreed—or faster.

What's the Point?

There are no shortcuts to building or rebuilding your credit. The secret is to pay your bills on time.

PART FOUR

The Home Dilemma

Your home is probably the largest purchase *and* the most important investment you will make. But as the housing bubble and bust of the 2000s proved, buying a home is not the financial sure thing many people thought it was. Even in good times, purchasing a home generates ongoing expenses, usually including a mortgage, which can double the purchase price. As an investment, a home creates some risk, provides no diversification, and often produces returns well below those of other investments.

The housing cycle of the 2000s left opportunities as well as lessons in its wake. In this part, I discuss housing decisions, and how they can have an impact on your wealth-building plans.

CHAPTER 13

Investing in Your Home

From the start of 1980 to the end of 2004, home sale
prices increased 247%. A pretty sweet deal, it would seem.
Over the same period, however, the S&P 500 shot up
more than 1,000%.
—Sara Clemence, editor and journalist

Homeownership has become such a badge of middle-class membership that what I'm about to say may seem counter-intuitive: You don't need to own your home to become wealthy. In fact, unless you handle homeownership wisely, it can undermine progress toward your financial goals. To avoid this result, you need to address these questions:

What role do you see your home playing in your investment plans?

Should you buy your home or rent?

These questions are significant because housing will probably be your largest living expense.

Investing in a Home

Over most of the past few decades, returns from home appreciation have been good and the risks reasonable. The housing bust that began in 2008 is a key exception.

It's tricky to compare owning a home to other investments. You can live in a house, which provides shelter for you and your family. You can't live in the S&P 500 index.

Many people find it comforting to know they will have their home paid for in retirement. Also, for some, mortgage payments represent "forced savings." As you pay your mortgage you *eventually* pay down principal and your equity grows.

The tax deductibility of mortgage interest subsidizes homeownership. This matters only if you are among the half of U.S. taxpayers who itemize deductions. Congress could change the rules for the tax deductibility of mortgage interest. If it did, the value of homes would likely decline.

A home also has disadvantages as an investment. The housing bust of the late 2000s and the poor market in subsequent years left millions of homeowners owing more on their mortgages than their homes were worth. Many people who lost their jobs also lost their homes. Others got stuck in homes they couldn't sell for the amounts they'd been counting on to fund their retirement.

Even without the housing bust, the *long-term* returns on housing generally fall well below returns on stocks.

Investment Returns: Your Home Versus the Stock Market

Comparing returns on housing and securities is difficult. Home prices in California, Las Vegas, Miami, and New York City skyrocketed in the 1990s and the early 2000s while many other areas saw normal appreciation. The dismal postrecession housing market also affected different areas in different ways.

All real estate is local, although few of us want to pick where we'll live based on expected price appreciation. There are also carrying costs with homeownership such as mortgage interest, property taxes, insurance, and maintenance.

As an investment, a home is not divisible. You can't sell your child's bedroom when he or she moves out. When you sell you also face substantial costs. However, you can sell as much of your portfolio as you want to, whenever you want to, with small transaction costs.

The most meaningful comparison of returns is based on broad measures over the long term. Short-term returns for all asset classes vary dramatically. For instance, between 2001 and 2006, home prices appreciated 12.4% annually according to the S&P/Case-Shiller Home Price Index for the United States while the S&P 500 gained only 4.3% annually.

> **mint hint**
>
> See the Mint.com real estate blog for solid information on buying and selling real estate (www.mint.com/invest/real-estate). Articles include "Should You Buy a Home Right Now?," "When's the Right Time to Sell?," and "How the Homeowner Bailouts Affect You."

"But over the long run stocks win easily," according to *Money Magazine* senior editor Marlys Harris. "A new study by Jack Clark Francis, a finance and economics professor at Baruch College in New York City, and Yale's Roger G. Ibbotson compared the annual returns of real estate from 1978 to 2004 with those of 15 different 'paper' investments. . . . The results? Housing delivered a solid but unimpressive annualized return of 8.6%. Commercial property did better at 9.5%. The S&P 500, however, delivered a crushing 13.4%."

Owning a home can be gratifying, but as an investment it is overrated when compared to a broadly diversified, periodically rebalanced portfolio of high-quality, low management fee stock and bond index funds. You may get lucky and sell your home for a substantial gain, but it is a gamble as an investment strategy.

What's the Point?

Don't view your home as a reliable investment that will fund your retirement.

CHAPTER 14

Home Economics: Should You Buy or Rent?

In the past, the government's financial and tax policies encouraged housing purchases.... Going forward, the government's primary role should be limited to robust oversight and consumer protection, targeted assistance for low- and moderate-income homeowners and renters....

—*Reforming America's Housing Finance Market:*
A Report to Congress, U.S. Department of the Treasury and
U.S. Department of Housing and Urban Development Paper
(February 2011)

In May 2010, a survey conducted by Harris Interactive found that 76% of those responding believed that renting was better than buying a home—up from 71% in 2008, the first year after the housing bust. Significantly, 78% of all the responders were homeowners. Maybe the grass looked greener when they bought their homes.

The "buy versus rent" decision is one to think about carefully. Here are the factors you need to consider.

The Price to Rent Ratio

When home prices skyrocketed during the 2000s housing bubble, many people became curious about renting versus buying.

A simple analysis can *help* you decide: the ratio of the price of a home to the annual rent of an equivalent home. It's not precise, but it's a good overall indicator.

Take the asking price of a home or the recent sales price of a similar home and divide it by the annual rent it would fetch. For example, if the price is $300,000 and the annual rent on a similar home is $18,000 (equal to $1,500/month times 12 months), the ratio is 16.67 or 17. This ratio is close to the U.S. national average for most of the past century, which was 16.

The higher the ratio—that is, the higher the purchase price is relative to the rent—the more it makes sense to rent. If that ratio decreases—that is, if prices decrease or rents increase—buying may make more sense. According to a 2010 *New York Times* article, based on Moody's Economy.com data, "When you do the math, you discover that a ratio above 20 means that you should at least consider renting, especially if you may move again in the next five years or so. When the ratio is well below 20, the case for buying becomes a lot stronger."

When home prices are rapidly rising or falling, the ratio in a location can change quickly. Also, future government policies may favor home buyers less, which may make renting more attractive.

Costs of Owning Versus Renting

The costs of homeownership include the down payment, closing costs, mortgage interest, insurance, maintenance, association fees, and property taxes. The renter incurs none of these costs, all of which are borne by the landlord. Homeowners accept higher costs for the benefits of ownership. Apart from pride of ownership and getting to customize your home and yard, the major benefit is price appreciation.

That brings us back to the investment element, discussed in Chapter 13. Even if you pay a reasonable price and see good appreciation, as an investment, a home may fail to match the returns on a balanced portfolio of low-cost stock and bond index funds. This difference in returns is another cost of homeownership.

What Can You Afford?

The three largest expenses most of us face are housing, food, and transportation. The ideal budgets in Chapter 6 allocated 20% to 25% of total income to housing and utilities. Many homeowners tend to underestimate the cost of owning. Based on the ideal budgets in Chapter 6, if you are at the 2010 U.S. household median income of $50,221, you can afford to spend $10,044 (20%) to $12,555 (25%) a year on housing. That's a range from $837 to $1,046 per month. In practice, many homeowners allocate 30% to 35% of their incomes to housing.

> ### mint hint
>
> Use Mint.com's free online monthly budget to determine how much you can afford to spend on housing (www.mint.com/free-online-financial-calculator). It will help you decide whether to rent or buy. If you want to buy but cannot afford to, look under the "Goals" tab for the "Buy a Home" goal. Mint will walk you through how much home you can afford based on your income, down payment, prevailing interest rates, and how far into the future you plan to buy.

Your income is what counts. You hope it will rise in the future. That means if you buy with a fixed-payment mortgage, your housing costs should diminish as a percentage of your income over the life of the loan. However, future earnings (and even employment) can be uncertain.

Regardless of your financial situation, there are numbers to crunch before you buy or rent a home.

What's the Point?

Calculate the price to rent ratio, costs of renting versus buying, and the amount you can afford to allocate to housing before you decide to rent or buy.

CHAPTER 15

Foreclosures and Short Sales

What's the outlook for home prices over the next decade? It's not easy to tell. We need to confront the basic fact that near the beginning of the 21st century, the market for homes in much of the world suddenly became more speculative than ever. This enormous bubble and burst isn't comparable to any national or international housing cycle in history.

—Robert J. Shiller, economist and author

The housing bust of the late 2000s generated 5 million foreclosures and, according to housing data firm CoreLogic, 11.1 million underwater homes (in which the amount of the mortgage exceeds the market value of the home). That underwater figure represents 23%—or nearly one-quarter—of all mortgaged homes in the United States. This is a problem that is going to be with us for a very long time.

News sources regularly carry stories of the great deals to be found in homes that have been subject to foreclosures and in short sales (where an underwater home sells for less than the mortgage, with the lender's approval). While you can certainly find attractive deals in today's weak housing market, even the most attractive ones typically present problems as well as opportunities. You *can* get into a home at a rock-bottom price, but it's never as straightforward as a usual sale.

The keys to success are to work with a real estate agent and an attorney with experience in these transactions. An experienced Realtor can locate these deals, and the attorney can represent your interest in negotiating and structuring the deal. This chapter gives you the information you need to know to have an informed discussion with these experts.

Foreclosures: Fraught with Pitfalls

When homeowners cannot pay their mortgages, lenders ultimately take possession of the property through agreement with the homeowner during preforeclosure or by buying the property at public auction. The lender writes off any unpaid mortgage principal that it can't recover.

Some real estate investors, often professionals, buy foreclosed properties at an auction held on the property site or at the courthouse. It's safer for the average person to buy a property from a bank that has recently foreclosed, according to Naples, Florida–based attorney Antonio Faga, who specializes in real estate.

The complexities in these deals involve knowing what to bid, having access to the property for inspection, and obtaining a "clean" title. Title issues are particularly critical, given well-publicized irregularities in some banks' foreclosure processes.

If you purchase the property at auction or through a sealed bid, you usually have 24 to 48 hours to come up with the cash. This means that you must have the money or have your financing lined up beforehand. It's generally more difficult to line up a traditional mortgage to purchase a foreclosure property.

For these reasons, a short sale may be a better option.

Short Sales: Proceed with Caution

A short sale occurs when an owner sells a house for less than the amount he owes on the mortgage. If you are the buyer, your concern is whether the bank will relinquish its lien or other security interest in the property and allow the sale to occur. Banks often (but not always) allow this when a homeowner is in arrears and cannot catch up. The bank gets most of the money it is owed and avoids the time, cost, and administrative work involved in foreclosure.

The seller negotiates with the bank to determine whether it will allow the sale to occur and forgive all or part of the difference between the sale price and the principal owed on the mortgage. (That difference is what makes it a "short sale.") The bank may forgive all of the unpaid balance or part of it and take the rest in future installments.

In many cases the bank approves the sale and allows the closing to occur, but reserves the right to pursue the seller for the remaining balance. When the deal is done correctly, the buyer still gets clear title and the bank pursues its claim for the remaining balance against the seller.

Watch Out!

Foreclosures and short sales are best suited to buyers who can be patient, who do not have to move into the home by a certain date, and who have cash or a large down payment (such as 50%). You

should work with professionals who have experience in foreclosures or short sales. Neither type of deal is a traditional closing.
Particularly in short sales, deal structures and administrative
details continue to change.

Before you make an offer on *any* condo, confirm that the association and the reserves are strong. When people walk away
from properties, the remaining owners often share increased
responsibility for maintenance, taxes, and other common costs.
Have an attorney experienced in the purchase and sale of condo-
miniums read the association's financial reports. Ask how many
people rent, how many owners live there, and how many units
have undergone foreclosure. If the association is weak or embat-
tled, avoid the property.

What's the Point?

There are bargains to be found in foreclosures and short sales, but
have a team of experts evaluate the risks and benefits before
proceeding.

CHAPTER 16

Outliving Your Mortgage

People are living longer than ever before, a phenomenon
undoubtedly made necessary by the 30-year mortgage.
—Doug Larson, columnist, *Green Bay Press-Gazette*

According to the U.S. Census Bureau, in 2009 almost
18.5 million owner-occupied dwellings belonged to people
65 and over. Of those, two-thirds were owned free and
clear. The other third were not. As the income of these seniors
declines, the monthly payments required by these mortgages
can imperil their quality of life.

That same survey revealed that almost 1.5 million seniors
owed $100,000 or more in mortgage principal. For all seniors
with mortgages, the median years left was 14—or about half the
length of the standard 30-year mortgage. When making your
long-term financial plan, ask yourself if you want to be paying
off your mortgage in your 70s. A shorter mortgage—or paying
off a longer-term one ahead of schedule—can be a good move.

The 30-year mortgage grew out of the Great Depression, when
the U.S. housing market needed help. Before then, people generally put down up to 50% of the price of the house and obtained a
mortgage for the rest. In the 1930s, the government made the
30-year, fixed-rate, 20% down mortgage the standard. It remained

the standard into the 1970s. The goal was to make housing more affordable. It did—by making it easier for people to carry deep debt for much of their lives.

Beginning in the 1970s, lower down payment and adjustable-rate mortgages (ARMs) became available, although 30-year, fixed-rate remained the most popular. Mortgage rates—and credit standards—reached new lows in the housing bubble of 2002 to 2007. Subprime loans, no-down-payment mortgages, and even interest-only mortgages all appeared. These mortgages caused problems for millions of homeowners—and, ultimately, for lenders as well.

Despite the bursting of the housing bubble, some "exotic" mortgages remain available. But when you take on long-term debt (a mortgage) in an uncertain market (housing) with high transaction costs (inspection, closing, and moving expenses), you should limit your risks. For that reason, I recommend a fixed-rate mortgage with a 20% minimum down payment, but not necessarily for 30 years.

Mortgage Madness

The lending industry has succeeded in getting borrowers to focus on the monthly payment. "Monthly affordability" comes at a high price. ARMs, graduated payment mortgages, no- or low-down-payment mortgages, and interest-only mortgages generally won't help your wealth-building efforts.

Fixed-rate mortgages with a fixed payment typically carry no prepayment penalty (but read the fine print). Know all your costs over the life of the mortgage before you sign.

An ARM exposes you to higher payments if rates rise. Graduated payment mortgages expose you to higher payments over time, and you're betting that your earnings will rise and other expenses will remain controlled. No- and low-down-payment loans increase your principal amount and interest expense. Interest-only mortgages have you pay interest but *no principal* for a period, say three or five years—a terrible idea even though the monthly payment is lower than for a mortgage that retires principal.

Remember, building wealth is about avoiding debt. The table below compares monthly payments and unamortized principal for a $200,000 loan at 5% interest at selected years for various terms using the mortgage calculator at money-zine.com. (To see your costs, use this calculator to plug in your own loan amounts, interest rates, and terms.)

As this table shows, the 30-year mortgage can be expensive. After 20 years of payments, more than $100,000—half the original amount—remains unpaid. That's because in the early years of the mortgage, most of the monthly payments go to interest expense. If you must take a 30-year mortgage, make an extra

KEY INFORMATION ON A $200,000 MORTGAGE AT 5% OVER 30-, 25-, 20-, AND 15-YEAR TERMS

Term of loan	30 years	25 years	20 years	15 years
Monthly payment	$1,073	$1,169	$1,320	$1,582
Total of payments	$386,512	$350,754	$316,779	$284,686
Total interest paid	186,512	150,754	116,779	84,686
Remaining principal . . .				
. . . Year 5	183,657	177,160	166,910	149,114
. . . Year 10	162,684	147,849	124,443	83,809
. . . Year 15	135,768	110,232	69,943	0
. . . Year 20	101,225	61,955	0	
. . . Year 25	56,893	0		
. . . Year 30	0			

payment (or two) every year. That requires discipline, but it's like having a shorter mortgage—you save interest expense and pay the loan off sooner.

In the long term, regardless of your home's appreciation, a shorter-term mortgage or extra payments increases your net worth by decreasing your debt and increasing your equity. Consequently, your wealth increases in ways that are far more certain than rising home prices.

What about a home as a hedge against inflation? Home prices usually rise during inflation, but so do mortgage rates, which can reduce demand for housing. The expectation of inflation is not a powerful reason to buy a home.

mint hint

See the article "Four Creative Financial Products That Got Us into Trouble" by Joshua Ritchie (and readers' comments) at the *MintLife* blog for interesting perspectives on home equity loans and biweekly mortgage payments (www.mint.com/blog/trends/home-equity-08182010). You can also check out Mint's mortgage calculator in their "Ways to Save" section, which will tell you whether now is the right time to refinance based on your home's current value and equity. If it is, Mint looks through several dozen mortgage providers to find the best rate based on your credit score.

Four Final Tips

- **Don't try to call the top or bottom.** Consider the age of any housing boom or bust, but don't base home-buying decisions on anticipated housing market movements.

- **Shop mortgages when you're in good financial shape.** Apply for a mortgage when your credit report will look good. If you've had a setback, rebuild your credit first.

- **Understand who's working for whom.** Real estate agents work for a commission on the sales price, paid by the seller, and benefit from a higher sales price.

- **Don't use your home as an ATM.** If you must take a home equity line to consolidate your loans, lower your interest, and get out of debt, that's one thing. But tapping the paper gains on your house erodes your wealth.

What's the Point?

When you minimize your monthly mortgage payment, you maximize the interest you pay. Carefully gauge the effect of any mortgage on your finances.

PART FIVE

Rest Insured: Solving the Insurance Rubik's Cube

The life insurance and healthcare insurance industries have assembled a bewildering line of products and plans. Most meet genuine needs, but too often the needs of the insurance company and its commissioned salespeople come first. The key issues for you are the types and amounts of life and health insurance you need—and the cost.

In this part, I examine your life and health insurance needs, products to consider and avoid, and how to get the best coverage at prices you can afford.

CHAPTER 17

The Term of Your Life

What the insurance companies have done is to reverse
the business so that the public at large insures the
insurance companies.
—Gerry Spence, attorney and author

A
sking a life insurance agent if you need more coverage is
like asking your barber if you need a haircut. Of course
you do. Nevertheless, there is ample support for the view
that most Americans are underinsured.

A 2010 survey by LIMRA (an organization with insurance
company members) found that half of U.S. households—the highest level ever—say they need more life insurance. This includes
one-third of households with $100,000 or more in annual income.
One in four households rely only on group life insurance (usually
from an employer), and only 44% have individual policies.
LIMRA estimates that 70% of U.S. households with children
under 18 would be in jeopardy if the primary breadwinner died.

The key life insurance questions for you as you create your
financial plan are these: Do you need life insurance? If so,
how much do you need? How long do you need it? After you
answer these questions you can consider what type of insurance
to buy.

Place Your Bet

All insurance is basically a bet. Something bad could happen that could have a financial impact on you or your loved ones—accident, illness, or death. An insurer creates a pool of insured individuals who pay premiums and, if or when the "something bad" happens, pays the benefit to the insured.

In life insurance, the payout is the death benefit (or the amount of coverage). Actuaries determine the premiums that will provide the policyholder's death benefit and cover the insurer's expenses and profit. The insurer invests those premiums to make money to pay the death benefit.

The death benefit is what you're buying when you buy term insurance, and it's a number you should calculate carefully. Term insurance pays a specific death benefit if you die during the term of coverage you purchase (for example, 10, 20, or 30 years), which is known as the *term* of the policy—hence the name *term insurance*. Unlike cash value life insurance, which I discuss in the next chapter, with term insurance your coverage and death benefit expire when the term of the policy expires.

Cash value insurance adds an investment component to the death benefit and potentially provides coverage for a lifetime. Even if you buy cash value insurance, you should know how much insurance coverage you want to buy.

Calculating Your Needs

If you are young or have no dependents, you may not need life insurance. If you plan to have dependents someday, life insurance can be worthwhile. If you buy it when you're young and healthy, you can guarantee that you will always be insurable (as long as you keep paying the premiums) regardless of your future medical condition.

Although you may hear that you should buy life insurance when you're young to lock in a low premium, that's not a good reason. Premiums are determined by your age, gender, and risk classification. Assuming you live to normal life expectancy, the younger you are, the more years you'll be paying the lower premiums. Similarly, the older you are, the fewer years you'll be paying the higher premiums.

What you have now doesn't have any bearing on what you need. Start with your current coverage (if any), regardless of when and how you obtained it. Then consider the two ways you can calculate your desired death benefit: an income-replacement approach or a needs-based approach.

Income-replacement approach: This approach mainly considers your age and earnings. For example, if you're 35 you may need 20 times your income. That would, in effect, cover 20 years of earnings. If you were to die 10 years after purchasing the policy, your survivors would have approximately the same sum as if you worked until age 65. To increase precision, some income-replacement calculations add up your projected after-tax earnings over your remaining working years, factor in inflation, and discount the results to current value. The income-replacement approach is not very individualized and generally produces a higher number than a needs-based approach.

Needs-based approach: A needs-based approach considers the impact of your death on your dependents and what you want to accomplish for them. This approach poses questions that pertain to you. Do you want your spouse not to have to work for 5, 10, or 15 years? If your spouse returned to work, would daycare be affordable? Is there a mortgage you'd want to pay off? Do you want to fund your children's college tuition? How much money do your survivors really need if you die? Could they handle the money responsibly? Would they use it as you intend? If not, perhaps you should set up a trust (as recommended in Part Ten). If the death benefit is to be invested, you may be able to project a rate of return on the invested amount, which could lower the coverage you'll need to buy.

A needs-based approach will give you a better idea of how much coverage you really need. It may require a little more thought, but it is the approach I recommend.

Is Term Insurance Right for You?

When you've calculated your death benefit, you can buy either term insurance or permanent insurance, with cash value being the most common type of permanent insurance. I will refer to permanent insurance as "cash value" insurance. There are many variants of each of these policies, which can make the decision about purchasing the right policy very confusing.

With term insurance you know exactly what you're buying because there's no investment component. You simply decide the amount of coverage and the period of time you want that coverage to be in effect and then compare rates for your age and health across reputable insurance companies.

With term life insurance you pay a level premium over the term of the policy (usually 10, 20, or 30 years). The younger you are and the shorter the term, the lower your premiums.

The complexity of cash value life insurance and its higher premiums (which I discuss in the next chapter) lead most financial advisers to say, "Buy term and invest the difference." But they're assuming you will actually invest the difference. Their advice may also be tainted by self-interest. If their fees are calculated by the amount of assets you *invest* with them, they may not be inclined to recommend paying higher premiums for a policy from which they will see no benefit.

My advice (in the next chapter) differs—because most people spend the difference. But seriously consider term insurance if you *need* the most affordable coverage available in the near term or, over the long term, you *know* that you will invest the difference.

Other Considerations

If your employer offers term life insurance, it may be good to opt in. Some employers pay part of the premium and, because you're in a group plan, premiums *may* be lower than those you could get as an individual. Always shop insurance and use insurers' websites as a starting point. Another option is to buy through an affiliate group, such as an alumni association or AARP. Savings bank life insurance (SBLI) has also historically been reliable and reasonably priced (www.sbli.com).

The key point is to seriously consider life insurance in your financial planning process. While term policies are sometimes preferable, there are many reasons to consider cash value policies, as explained in Chapter 18. Note this: More than

mint hint

Mint.com provides a life insurance wizard, which uses your age, annual income, and whether you own a home and have dependents to estimate your needed coverage (https://www.mint.com/life-insurance). The wizard also provides some life insurance companies so you can compare quotes.

90% of term policies never pay a death benefit because often it becomes too expensive for the policyholder to maintain coverage.

What's the Point?

A needs-based analysis is the best way to determine how much life insurance coverage you require.

CHAPTER 18

Cash Value Life Insurance

When it comes to cash value insurance, I can't think of any other
arena where the difference between a great product and a
horrible one can go unrecognized by all of the participants
for decades.

—Scott Witt, fee-only insurance adviser

Welcome to one of the most confusing topics in personal
finance: cash value life insurance. Cash value insurance
can be an excellent product, but its complexity makes it
hard to understand that value. That complexity favors insurance
salespeople, who tend to sell the policies that pay them the highest commission.

The two main types of cash value life insurance are whole life
insurance and universal life insurance, and they work similarly.
The premiums for both are higher than for term insurance with
a similar death benefit, and a portion of the higher premiums is
invested so the policy accrues cash value. A high percentage of
the first year's premium (50% or more) goes to the salesperson as
a commission. This gives salespeople strong incentives to sell
cash value policies.

Whole Life

The main features of whole life are:

- You pay a level premium for a set period of time, often for life.

- You have no control over the investment component.

- When you die, your beneficiaries receive the death benefit in the policy at the time of your death.

Your beneficiaries do not receive the cash value at the time of your death—only the death benefit. If dividends are used to increase the cash value over a number of years, then at some point you will have enough value in the policy to pay future premiums.

Whole life generally has higher premiums than universal life because it guarantees a death benefit, a level premium, and a guaranteed growth rate in cash value. If you pay your premiums, your policy will remain in force for life. You pay more for the guaranteed death benefit and guaranteed cash value.

Universal Life

The main features of universal life are:

- Your premium payments are more flexible because you pay for the cost of the life insurance and then contribute as much as you like to the investment component.

- You have no control over how the investment component is invested unless you have a variable policy, in which case you can select options from those offered by the insurer.

- You can choose to have the premiums paid completely out of your accumulated returns when you have a high enough balance on the policy.

Universal life has lower premiums than whole life because the death benefit can vary due to fluctuations in investment performance and the cash value is not guaranteed. The advantage of universal life is "premium flexibility"—premiums are *automatically* deducted from the cash value if you miss your payments.

Cash value policies are a significant financial investment. I strongly recommend you consult a fee-only insurance adviser if you are considering insurance with an annual premium of $2,500 or more. These advisers are paid a flat fee for their advice and don't benefit from any decision you make about life insurance. They can be objective. In contrast, the primary loyalty of the life insurance salesperson is to the insurance company. I provide a list of fee-only insurance advisers in Part Twelve, where I give the resources for this and all other chapters.

Approach Cash Value Policies Cautiously

Here are a few things that can trip you up when choosing a cash value policy:

Variations on policies: The options for cash value policies are mind-boggling and include graded-premium, interest-sensitive, and modified-premium *and* participating, variable, and single-premium whole life. Types of universal life include no-lapse, indexed, and variable. Without a fee-paid adviser, you must depend on insurance salespeople, who have conflicts of interest, to explain which is best for you.

Unequal treatment of policyholders: Some companies offer high guarantees to new customers by, in effect, raiding their current policyholders' funds. This occurs more in stock than in mutual insurance companies. A stock company has both policyholders and shareholders, while the mutual company has only policyholders (who own the company). You may get a good deal on a guaranteed policy from a stock company making aggressive guarantees, but do *not* buy a nonguaranteed policy from a stock company. If the stock company becomes financially stressed, your nonguaranteed policy may fail to deliver projected returns because the company must first pay guaranteed returns.

Costs and returns: Insurance companies have sales and administrative costs, paid for by premiums. Having an insurer invest your money is like having an active fund manager do it. You face higher fees and lower returns than you would with the arrangements I'll discuss in Parts Six and Seven.

But there are still very good reasons for buying cash value insurance.

What's Good About Cash Value Insurance?

Like homeownership, cash value life insurance encourages forced savings. People do let insurance policies lapse, but there's a strong incentive to keep paying premiums to keep your death benefit in place.

Between whole and universal life, whole life is preferable if you know you'll be able to pay the premiums and don't foresee swings in your desired death benefit. You'll usually get a higher return than on universal life. On the other hand, if you want greater premium flexibility, universal is preferable.

You might consider a blended policy, which combines whole life and term life into a single policy. A blended policy should generate higher near-term cash values and higher death benefits at life expectancy than whole life alone because of lower sales costs. Your insurance agent might not mention these policies because the commissions are much lower than other options, but they are sold by many highly rated companies, including North-western Mutual, Guardian, New York Life, and Mass Mutual.

There are many inferior cash value policies, both in force and being sold today. The differences between superior and inferior cash value policies are significant. You should seriously consider retaining a fee-only insurance adviser, with no financial stake in your purchase decision, to be sure the policy you buy is the best one available for you.

Finally, there's another, returns-driven reason to buy cash value insurance. According to fee-only insurance adviser Scott Witt, an in-surance expert can assemble a portfolio of cash value policies that will rival a portfolio of fixed-income investments. The insurance will also provide a death benefit, which an investment portfolio does not. It's possible to put your entire fixed-income exposure in cash value life insurance. "If properly structured it may never go down," Witt notes, "and it can allow you to be far more aggressive in the balance of your portfolio."

> **mint hint**
>
> Mint.com provides useful articles on life insurance, like "How Much Is Your Life Worth? Life Insurance 101" (www.mint.com/blog/how-to/life-insurance-101).

The *only* part of your portfolio that cash value life insurance can replace is fixed income. Cash value policies cannot generate returns comparable to those of equities. But they *can*—subject to the caveats in this chapter—produce a higher after-tax yield with less volatility than a fixed-income portfolio.

What's the Point?

Cash value life insurance can be a useful financial planning tool
if you have a fee-only insurance adviser to help you choose
the best one for your needs.

CHAPTER 19

Annuities: Don't Toss the Baby Out with the Bathwater

They [variable annuities] are arguably among the more costly,
oversold options available.
—Barbara Roper, director of investor protection,
Consumer Federation of America

The popularity of annuities surged in the late 2000s recession. Smartmoney.com reported that 2009 sales of fixed annuities (I'll explain what these are) reached $108 billion— up 48% over 2007 levels. The report added, "But with much of the business dominated by insurance agents and financial planners, it is notoriously difficult to comparison shop."

An annuity is a financial product where the buyer pays a lump sum or a stream of payments to the company selling the annuity. The company invests that money and, on a specified date, pays a lump sum or begins a stream of payments to the buyer or beneficiary.

The period when the payments are made to the insurance company is the accumulation phase. The period when the buyer receives payments from the insurance company is the distribution (or income) phase. You're usually not required to have the annuity at the same company in each phase, which many buyers don't realize. At the end of the accumulation phase, you can cash in the annuity, pay the applicable taxes, engage in a tax-free exchange for another annuity (known as a "1035 Exchange"), or buy another annuity with that company or another one.

Annuities can be among the worst deals in the financial marketplace—complex, high-cost, low-return investment products. If you intend to buy one, get advice from a fee-only insurance adviser.

Key Types of Annuities

Deferred annuity: You make regular payments to the insurance company, which invests your money and, at maturity, starts making payments to you or your beneficiary. The goal is to accumulate savings and returns for the company to distribute to you later in life, with taxes on the returns deferred. Generally, the rate of return will be well below what you could earn over a similar period on a balanced portfolio of equities (as explained in Parts Six and Seven). Deferred annuities can offer a fixed, variable, or indexed rate of return.

Variable annuity: These let you invest in specific funds, which vary by insurer. If you die, these annuities pay at least the total of your contributions (less any withdrawals) to your beneficiaries. This is the case even if the annuity's value is lower than your contributions when you die. That sounds attractive, but it's not a reason to buy these annuities. They feature high costs—averaging about 2% annually—and for a specific period you can't pull your money out without penalties.

Equity indexed annuity: These offer a guaranteed rate of return *and* allow for upside gains in a rising stock market. The guaranteed return will generally be lower than for a comparable immediate annuity, but the upside potential attracts buyers. These annuities are usually tied to a market index like the S&P 500. But their complexity hides features that lower your returns. An insurer can even change contract provisions after you sign up. Surrender periods typically last 10 to 17 years with early withdrawal penalties up to 10% to 12% of your money.

Immediate annuity: You pay a lump sum and soon start receiving monthly, quarterly, or annual payments for the rest of your life (hence the "immediate"). The goal is to obtain a higher rate of return than on a savings account or CD and to have a guaranteed income, usually for the rest of your life—or most of it. Inflation-protected annuities (IPAs) are similar to immediate annuities but the payments are indexed to the rate of inflation. While IPAs are more expensive (when compared with noninflation-protected immediate annuities), I believe their benefits in eliminating (or reducing) inflation risk makes them a valuable option for investors.

Immediate *variable* annuities typically offer a guaranteed income and upside potential. However, if you're seeking upside potential, you can allocate your assets in your portfolio (as explained in Parts Seven and Eight) to achieve higher returns without the costs of an annuity. An immediate *fixed* annuity provides a known income stream and no exposure to loss of principal.

"Immediate annuities are under-utilized," says insurance adviser Scott Witt, "because people fear that if they buy an immediate annuity and die tomorrow, all is lost. Insurers try to address this with features such as minimum years of payments and spousal benefits, but that erodes the returns. If you want to not outlive your income, there's no tool more powerful than a regular immediate annuity."

You can use an immediate annuity to pay yourself a "pension" to supplement your Social Security payments, an IRA, or an actual pension. Vanguard and TIAA-CREF are the industry leaders in low-cost immediate annuities.

Intelligent Annuity Choices

Variable annuities of all stripes tend to be bad deals. Equity indexed annuities are my least favorite. The complexity of these products leaves consumers dependent on salespeople who usually fail to fully explain tax consequences, expenses, and withdrawal penalties. In many cases, the salespeople don't understand the product they are selling.

Salespeople do tout the tax deferral benefits of a variable annuity but don't mention that the withdrawals are taxed as ordinary income. True, you won't have to pay tax on money in an annuity until it's withdrawn, but if the money were in a taxable mutual fund for more than a year, it would be taxed at the capital gains rate, which has historically been lower than the income tax rate.

Annuity payouts can spread out income and thus mitigate income taxes, and a portion of the payout is return of (already taxed) principal rather than taxable income. But mutual funds give you more flexibility and far lower expenses, which are usually unreasonably high with a variable annuity.

Variable annuities should generally be avoided. I have never seen any justification for owning an annuity within a retirement plan. You are paying a premium for a tax deferral benefit you already have within the plan.

In stark contrast, immediate annuities can play an important role in your retirement planning. The primary reason they are underused in retirement planning can be traced to the conflict of interest of brokers and advisers, who get compensated based on assets under management. The purchase of an immediate annuity reduces these assets, which means lower fees for them. You need to proactively determine whether an immediate annuity (and especially an inflation-protected immediate annuity) is right for you.

What's the Point?

In general, it's best to avoid annuities, except for immediate fixed annuities.

CHAPTER 20

Health Insurance

**If I bought groceries the way I buy health insurance, I'd eat a lot
better—and so would my dog.**
—Phil Gramm, U.S. senator

When you're ill or injured, you want the care you need.
Everyone knows this. Yet the nonsense spewed forth
about healthcare and health insurance—mostly from
those who profit from the current system or who represent those
who do—never seems to end.

To get healthcare you need Medicare or private insurance or
you go to the emergency room and get billed. Most people (85%)
on Medicare are satisfied, and 67% are as or more satisfied as
they were with their previous, employer-sponsored plans. But
you can't get Medicare until you are 65, and the program could
be affected by future legislation. (Medicaid is the state-level program for the needy.)

Your insurance can affect your healthcare. Your plan must
offer access to reputable, expert caregivers. You also have to
advocate for yourself with your caregivers and insurer, or have
someone advocate for you. If you or a friend can't do it, consider
hiring a professional patient advocate. You can find them at
AdvoConnection (www.advoconnection.com/index.asp) and

the National Association for Home Care & Hospice (www.nahc
.com). Never go without health insurance, and be careful what
you buy.

Key Types of Plans

Broadly speaking, there are indemnity plans and managed care
plans.

Indemnity plans allow you to choose your healthcare providers, with the insurer picking up most of the tab (usually 80%)
and, usually, a cap on your annual out-of-pocket costs. Indemnity plans (like traditional Blue Cross Blue Shield) have been
largely priced out of the market because they generate the highest costs for insurers.

Managed care plans—mainly preferred provider organizations
(PPOs) and health maintenance organizations (HMOs)—control
costs by controlling access to care. The insurer assembles a network of providers and negotiates rates with them for visits and
procedures. The insurer usually requires a referral from your
primary care provider (PCP) to see a specialist and limits the fre-
quency of certain tests.

A PPO usually offers more choice and access than an HMO.
HMOs more strictly limit access to out-of-network providers. A
PPO charges a set co-pay (usually $10 to $25) for a visit and
in-office procedures. If you go out of network, you may need a
referral from your PCP or pay a higher co-pay or both.

A point-of-service (POS) plan provides the option of going out
of network without a referral, but at a higher co-pay or on an
indemnity model.

With any healthcare plan, you *must* understand what will and
won't be covered as well as your financial exposure.

Key Questions to Ask

First, review the plan's list of doctors and hospitals at its website and ensure that the network includes those you like and trust. Then ask the following:

- What is the monthly or annual premium? Do I qualify for any discounts?

- What do I pay for each visit? Which procedures are—and aren't—covered? What do I pay for those not covered?

- What referrals do I need to see a specialist and to go out of network?

- What is the deductible—the annual amount I must pay to providers before coverage kicks in?

- What is the maximum amount I'll pay for healthcare in a year (the stop-loss)?

- What is the definition of a preexisting condition? To what extent are preexisting conditions covered?

- What in-home equipment, such as a wheelchair, is and isn't covered?

- Is there a prescription drug benefit? If so, what is covered and what are my costs? If not, what would it cost to get that coverage?

Ask these questions regardless of how or where you purchase health insurance. Be particularly careful if you are self-employed and buying insurance on your own. If you are self-employed, investigate affiliate groups like professional associations, which often offer access to health insurance at group rates. However, be sure you understand the policies well because affiliate groups usually do not negotiate as aggressively on behalf of their members as employers do for employees, nor do they subsidize premiums. If you leave your employment, consider buying health insurance via COBRA.

Buying via COBRA

The Consolidated Omnibus Budget Reconciliation Act (COBRA) allows former employees to purchase—for up to 18 months *at their own expense but at the employer's group rate*—the coverage they had while employed. In many cases, your spouse and dependent children may be eligible for COBRA coverage for as long as three years.

COBRA premiums can be extremely high, so consider the alternatives before signing up (though you can drop the coverage whenever you choose). COBRA generally does not apply to companies with fewer than 20 employees in the prior year, and your company HR representative or healthcare insurer is generally the best source for information.

Catastrophic Health Insurance

Catastrophic health insurance plans provide high deductibles and lower premiums. Under a high-deductible health plan (HDHP) you pay for visits, procedures, and hospitalizations up to a high amount. The minimum deductible can be as low as $1,100 for an individual or $2,200 for a family, but can reach $3,000 to $5,000 or more.

HDHP is for people who can't afford the high premiums of

plans with low deductibles, yet assumes they can pay the high deductible. In practice, people with these plans often forgo routine care and hope they don't fall ill. Yet an HDHP does limit your exposure to catastrophic health care bills, so don't rule it out. You can learn more about HDHPs at the High-Deductible Health Insurance website (www.high-deductible-health-insurance.org). Also see IRS Publication 969, titled "Health Savings Accounts (HSA) and Other Tax-Favored Health Plans." (You must be enrolled in an HDHP to qualify for a HSA.)

Government Programs and Other Options

As noted, Medicare and Medicaid are the two major government healthcare programs. Medicare information can be found at www.medicare.gov. Medicaid is run by the states for lower-income residents. Check your state's official website for information.

You may have other government-sponsored options. Former members of the military have the Veterans Administration. You may qualify for a high-risk pool of otherwise uninsurable individuals in

> **mint hint**
>
> Mint.com offers articles on choosing healthcare insurance, such as "How to Choose a Health Insurance Plan That Works for You" (www.mint.com/blog/how-to/choosing-a-health-insurance-plan), and related topics, like "Health Care Reformed: What Will Change for You?" (www.mint.com/blog/trends/health-care-reform).

your state. Visit your state's website and search on healthcare options. It is also possible that a short-term (three-, six-, or nine-month) plan with a private insurer may cover you between jobs at affordable rates.

In addition, consider dental insurance, which may seem like a luxury but can save you the expensive, painful complications that come with lack of dental care. Delta Dental Plans, the largest U.S. dental care insurer, operates in all 50 states. Check them out at www.deltadental.com.

What's the Point?

Devote the time and effort required to find affordable health insurance—and never go without it.

The Investment Industry: Friend and Foe

Investment companies can either facilitate or undermine your wealth-building efforts, depending on how you use them. Investment companies make the capital markets possible and offer investment vehicles that can help you build wealth. Unfortunately, they have also intensified their efforts to separate you from your money.

Part Six shows how the investment industry makes money, what to avoid, and how little the industry has changed—even after the financial crisis of the late 2000s. The next three parts are extremely important to your wealth-building efforts. The object of budgeting, avoiding debt, and making the right real estate and insurance decisions is to have money to invest. When you have that money, you then have to make it work as hard as possible.

CHAPTER 21

Goldman Sachs: Paragon or Pariah?

Morningstar Inc. tracks Goldman mutual funds and found that the 338 fund share classes it looks at trailed the average return of their respective peers in every broad category . . . over the 3-, 5-, and 10-year periods ended on Dec. 31. Yet investors have not only stuck with [Goldman funds]; they've added tens of billions of dollars to its assets since 2000.

—Richard Teitelbaum, financial journalist

Investment bank Goldman Sachs has been compared unfairly to a "great vampire squid" stuck on the face of humanity sucking out anything that smells like money. The harsh reality is that *every* investment company operates like Goldman, though usually less successfully. Perhaps its success at profiting in all circumstances, exploiting all sides of the deals it creates, and launching so many of its alumni into politics has caused Goldman Sachs to become the whipping boy of the securities industry.

In the 1980s and 1990s, all the major investment banks converted from partnerships to corporations. That gave them access to vast amounts of shareholders' money. This massive infusion of funds encouraged these banks to increase their debt and to place larger, riskier bets. Those factors helped create the financial crisis of 2007–2008.

The Greatest Investment Scam Ever

With very few exceptions, every investment company assures its customers that its actively managed funds outperform the market and that they should pay for that performance. Every year, investment companies collectively sell thousands of these funds and charge millions in fees on this basis.

Though it may seem hard to believe, this is a Wall Street scam because these funds *do not* consistently outperform their respective indexes. Over the long term, passively managed funds—specifically, low-cost index funds—almost invariably outperform actively managed funds.

Consider:

- Actively managed funds typically aim to "beat the market" or, more accurately, a designated market index. Yet long term, more than 95% of actively managed mutual funds fail to equal or beat their market indexes.

- Actively managed funds cost more—on average about 1.5% of the assets being managed versus 0.35% or less for most index funds—which erodes investors' returns. Transaction costs further eat into returns. From an investor's perspective, this difference in costs is the primary reason that index funds outperform actively managed funds.

- Actively managing your own portfolio, rather than investing in a globally diversified portfolio of low management fee index funds or using a passive adviser to assist you in doing so, reduces returns, generates risks, increases stress,

and uses time that could be put to more enjoyable (and profitable) uses.

How Do They Get Away with It?

Hundreds of studies have demonstrated that the vast majority of
actively managed funds *underperform* the market. These are
research studies based on sound historical data analyzed by
objective observers in academic finance.

If that's so, how do brokers and financial advisers get away
with selling actively managed funds at higher costs to investors?

There are two main reasons. First, very expensive and effective advertising and sales efforts continually transmit the message that active fund managers regularly beat market returns and
can do so in the future. In 2010, the industry ranked fifth among
U.S. industries in ad spending with $7.7 billion across all media. It
was outranked only by automotive, telecom, local services, and
retail. Financial services outranked personal care products, restaurants, and pharmaceuticals. It takes a lot of money to persuade
you to buy something that makes little financial sense.

Second, people *want* to believe that message. These two factors fuel the majority of investment decisions—and the financial
services industry makes money from every trade, just as a casino
makes money on every game.

The media stand ready to
enhance this advertising. Endless
"news" stories about market ups
and downs, hot and cold stocks,
stellar CEOs, and so-called Wall
Street gunslingers—and features
on stock and fund picking, options
trading, and investing in gold,

mint hint

See the article "Pitched These Investment Products? Just Say No"
by Matthew Amster-Burton (www
.mint.com/blog/investing/where
-not-to-invest-06222010).

commodities, and so on—aim to keep investors in a state of panic and anxiety.

While their clients suffer from following advice that has little to support it, brokers and others in the securities industry continue to prosper. Bonuses paid to New York City employees in the financial securities industry amounted to $20.8 billion in 2010.

What's the Point?

Most investment companies work a perfectly legal scam. They falsely and repeatedly claim they can beat the market, and gullible investors believe them.

CHAPTER 22

The Fix Is (Still) In

Wall Street did not produce much leadership during its darkest
hour [the early 1930s]. . . . When asked about solutions to the
depression, Albert Wiggin of Chase told *Time* that perhaps the
Sherman Anti-Trust Act should be eased.

—Charles R. Geisst, author of *Wall Street: A History*

The financial crisis of 2007–2008 initiated, by most measures, the longest, most severe recession in the United States
since the Great Depression. Massive debt and falling home
prices resulted directly from banking, mortgage lending, and
investing practices that transformed what could have been a normal, cyclical recession into a near depression.

During the crisis, the U.S. Treasury provided some $750 bil-
lion to banks to stabilize the financial markets under the Troubled Asset Relief Program (TARP), passed during the final
months of George W. Bush's administration. TARP also *required*
the Treasury to provide relief for distressed homeowners. Yet
widespread relief for homeowners (aka taxpayers) never materialized although more than 5 million foreclosures from 2007
through 2010 did.

From 2009 through 2011, the industry which taxpayers bailed
out fought reform tooth and nail. The industry won, thanks to

the revolving door between Wall Street and Washington, the power of lobbyists and campaign contributions, and the perception (in some quarters) that true reform was unnecessary. As a result, the misnamed Wall Street Reform and Consumer Protection Act ("Dodd-Frank") left the structure and practices that led to the crisis largely in place.

Investors can take three valuable—though hardly new— lessons from this.

Lesson 1: Nothing Changes on Wall Street

The 1920s were rife with investment industry chicanery, and so were the 2000s. In the 2000s, after abandoning long-standing credit policies, the mortgage industry resold—through investment banks—over a *trillion* dollars worth of subprime mortgages, usually as highly rated securities. Those mortgage-backed securities (MBS) received high bond ratings because the rating agencies are paid by the companies that issue the bonds being rated—a clear conflict of interest.

That rating system remains in place, largely because the three major bond-rating agencies—Standard & Poor's, Moody's, and Fitch—successfully fought any meaningful reform that would have affected the conflict-ridden way they do business. These entities are neither government agencies nor "agencies" in any other real sense of the term. They make their money (and lots of it) by charging fees to the companies whose bonds they rate.

No investment banking or ratings agency executives were prosecuted or even charged. Indeed, they opposed regulations designed to curb future abuses and to protect consumers. Dodd-Frank calls mainly for greater disclosure and modest regulation of derivatives, the instruments Warren Buffett called "financial weapons of mass destruction," but leaves the industry largely undisturbed.

Lesson 2: The Industry Sides with the Industry

A number of sales, fee-generating, and fund management practices of investment companies are reprehensible, yet investors have little recourse. The Financial Industry Regulatory Authority (FINRA) settles disputes between investors and brokers. FINRA is not a government agency, but rather an industry-sponsored "self-regulatory" body. The FINRA "mandatory arbitration system" embodies another conflict of interest because industry-sponsored regulators cannot objectively resolve these disputes.

When FINRA arbitration panels find that its member brokers have damaged an investor by their misconduct, it usually "awards" the investor partial recovery of the fees or losses that should not have occurred in the first place. These awards are viewed by the brokerage firm as a small cost of doing business. There is no deterrent to future misconduct.

FINRA was created in 2007 by merging the National Association of Securities Dealers and the enforcement arm of the New York Stock Exchange. In 2005, the predecessor agencies collected $137 million in fines, but by 2009, that figure had fallen to $38 million. The merger clearly accomplished its goals. Brokers and their firms can engage in a broad range of misconduct, without fear of any effective sanctions from FINRA. It is a very cozy system—for everyone but investors.

Lesson 3: The Government Has Abandoned Consumers

Any hope that a global financial crisis would prompt the U.S. government to institute new safeguards for consumers has evaporated. Banks that are "too big to fail" remain in place, as does myopic oversight by boards of directors and toothless regulation by Washington.

There are logical arguments against limiting the size of banks.

Large banks can provide some services at lower costs and compete more effectively against large foreign banks. But should they be able to, as economist Paul Krugman puts it, privatize their profits and socialize their losses?

Over the past 40 years financial services companies have seen massive deregulation and tremendous growth, while household income and consumer savings have stagnated. Neither the industry nor its "overseers" in the legislative or executive branches have exhibited more than token interest in the welfare of consumers or individual investors.

After the Crash of 1929 and during the Great Depression, the United States enacted vast reform of the investment industry. Many of those regulations were repealed or left unenforced from the 1970s through the 2000s. After the global financial crisis of the late 2000s, serious reforms were not enacted nor were useful regulations reinstated, which goes to show how powerful the lobby for the financial services industry has become. The way I view it, the financial services industry has "equity" in Congress. It's been a great investment.

> ### mint hint
>
> For more views on the financial crisis and financial industry reform, see Mint.com's *MintLife* blog posts tagged "financial crisis" (www.mint.com/blog/tag/financial-crisis). Articles include "Four Creative Financing Products That Got Us in Trouble," "How Banks Prey on Their Customers," and "The Financial Reform Bill Highlights the Need for Real Reform."

What's the Point?

The financial services industry profits from boom-and-bust cycles, but it's a far more depressing story for investors, consumers, and homeowners.

CHAPTER 23

Wall Street's Casinos

We are all wrong so often that it amazes me that we can
have any conviction at all over the direction of things to come.
But we must.
—Jim Cramer, host of *Mad Money*, CNBC

If you search the web for "roulette system," you'll find sites
offering ways to win at roulette. One system notes that of the 36
numbers on the wheel, in any 36 spins only 15 to 20 different
numbers come up. Thus some numbers come up multiple times
in 36 spins. The "system" is to use the electronic list of recent
spins posted near the wheel to choose a likely number to play
until it hits again (for a 36 to 1 payout). Another system is to bet
red or black (a two-to-one payout) and double your bet until you
win big or lose your budgeted money.

Some of these sites give their systems away, while others sell
them. Do you think the systems that cost money are better than
the free ones? If so, you may have money invested in actively
managed mutual funds.

As businesses, casinos rig the games in their favor. Unfortunately, so do most investment companies. However, I am *not*
equating investing with gambling or smart investors with gamblers. In fact, some gamblers are smart. Unlike casual players, they

set reasonable goals, know the odds on the game they're playing, understand the house's advantage, and use money management systems to limit their losses (which is all a roulette system can do).

You would think most investors would do the same. You would be wrong.

The Markets Set the Odds

The stock and bond markets are not casinos, though they're often compared with them. The markets enable public companies to access investors' funds and allow investors to buy stocks and bonds. A stock is an ownership share in a company—a share in the company's future profits. A bond is essentially an agreement for the company to pay interest and principal on long-term borrowings.

Legally, the stockholder is an owner of the company and the bondholder is a creditor. This is not like betting on the turn of a wheel or a card. There's a lot less chance involved. As I'll explain in Part Seven, there's even less chance involved when you purchase index funds because your money is invested in many companies rather than in one, two, or several.

However, investors do put money at risk. That's why they earn higher returns than savers. This element of risk causes people to compare the markets with casinos.

But in the world of investing the real casinos are the investment companies.

Las Vegas Meets Wall Street

Here are five ways in which casinos and investment companies are alike:

Mixed messages: Each industry rarely mentions money explicitly because they don't want you thinking about losing it. Casinos emphasize stage shows, food, booze, luxury, and Sin City swagger—and, by the way, we have gambling. Investment companies talk about your future and security—occasional tugging your heartstrings—and tout their expertise, experience, and trustworthiness. Both industries downplay risks and costs.

Action and activity: In advertisements and other marketing efforts, both industries emphasize action and activity. They have hot tables or hot funds, superior payouts or buying opportunities, all geared to creating excitement and the expectation of big wins. Each industry makes money on transactions—bets or buy-and-sell decisions—and if you're not making them, the place is dead.

Big perks for whales and elephants: Whales are the big gamblers coveted by casinos. Win or lose, whales get complimentary rooms, food, drinks, and transportation. High net worth individuals are known as elephants at one major trust company, which designates certain salespeople as elephant hunters. These giant financial mammals are also wined and dined and get news of "special situations" available only to "sophisticated investors."

A veneer of regulation: Three words: *Nevada Gaming Commission*. Four more: *Securities and Exchange Commission*. The former allows people to buy chips on credit in casinos. The latter allows FINRA to settle disputes between brokers and investors and to engage in purported self-regulation of the securities industry. In both cases, foxes are minding the chicken coop.

Money magnets: The goal of each industry is to separate you from your money. Cynics might say that's every industry's goal.

mint hint

You can educate yourself about investing with Mint.com's videos. Titles have included Burton G. Malkiel's *How to Invest Your Money*, Zina Spezakis's *A Guide to Mutual Funds*, and Jason Zweig's *Being Cautious in Your Investments*.

But there is a critical difference: Most enterprises provide something of known value in exchange for your money—houses, cars, food, clothing, flights to distance places, coronary bypasses, whatever. Gaming and investing offer the prospect of doubling your money without much effort. If you lose, you have nothing to show for it. Most gamblers and many investors find themselves in precisely that situation.

Because the markets set the odds, you can have a very good idea of the risks you are taking, as I explain in Part Seven. But first, there is one more pitfall to avoid: salespeople posing as advisers.

What's the Point?

The way most people invest is akin to gambling—with similar results.

CHAPTER 24

Advice About Advisers

I do not regard a broker as a member of the human race.
—Honoré de Balzac, French novelist

Investment salespeople dealing with individual investors very rarely refer to themselves as salespeople. Instead, they cast themselves as brokers, agents, financial planners, financial consultants, investment managers, account executives, vice presidents, and other impressive titles. The reality is they are salespeople—nothing more.

Salespeople exist to overcome resistance, and investment salespeople don't want you even thinking about resisting. They work on commission or bury their fees in transactions or charge you a percentage of your assets or deduct fees from your returns.

Are brokers really offering "advice" as that term is understood by clients of attorneys, accountants, and similar professionals? Often a broker's advice simply generates transactions (and commissions).

Brokers work for the brokerage firms that employ them, not for you. Their primary loyalty is to their employer.

Investment advisers (also known as Registered Investment

Advisors), who charge for their advice *and* stand to gain no commission, finder's fee, origination fee, transfer fee, or other fees based on *your* financial decisions, *are* fee-only advisers. Their primary allegiance is to you. They are not permitted to have any interests that conflict with yours.

If you need an adviser, you should avoid brokers and deal only with Registered Investment Advisors. Here's a litmus test: Ask them to state in writing that they have a "fiduciary obligation to you." This means they can have no interests in conflict with yours. Registered Investment Advisors will gladly make this representation. Brokers won't.

Do You Need an Adviser?

Whether you need an adviser is a very personal decision. If you have the time and inclination, it is certainly possible to manage your own investments. In *The Smartest Investment Book You'll Ever Read* and *The Smartest Portfolio You'll Ever Own*, I tell you exactly how to do so, including the specific mutual funds you should purchase.

The guidelines in Part Eight provide all the investment advice you'll need to start investing properly. Even if you don't need an adviser, the right one can help you set a course toward financial freedom regardless of your current situation.

If you have significant assets (more than $250,000) and life insurance needs, you need an advisory team. This team should include an independent Registered Investment Advisor (RIA), an *independent* estate planning attorney, a certified public accountant (CPA), and a fee-only insurance adviser.

Be sure each member of your team is really independent. They can *recommend* products, provided they receive no compensation, but even that may be dicey. For instance, in return for mutual referrals (with no money changing hands) there are estate planning attorneys who recommend certain insurance salespeople and vice versa. Be sure you ask about these relationships and obtain multiple referrals.

What Investment Advisers Do

The *right* adviser can help you by:

- Answering questions, explaining financial matters, and helping you formulate your goals and understand your risk profile.

- Determining, with you, your asset allocation (the division of your portfolio between stocks, bonds, and cash), given your goals, needs, and risk profile, and helping you to select low management fee index funds, passively managed funds, or exchange traded funds for your portfolio.

- Working with you to rebalance your portfolio once or twice a year.

- Keeping you from selling in down markets, or getting greedy in bull markets, by keeping your portfolio in an asset allocation appropriate for you.

- Engaging in tax loss harvesting when appropriate.

RIAs should provide a written agreement setting forth their fee structure and other details regarding the services they will be providing to you.

Who Can You Turn To?

Here are three rules to help you choose the right investment adviser:

- Avoid anyone who says he can beat the market—or that he has consistently beaten it—and anyone who wants to pick individual stocks or bonds for you.

- Avoid anyone who doesn't give you straight answers about his relationships with financial services companies and about how he bills and how he is paid.

- Avoid anyone who will not agree to use *exclusively* low management fee index funds, EFTs, or passively managed funds instead of actively managed funds in your portfolio.

RIAs must register with the SEC or their state. However, that does not guarantee their competence or expertise, especially if they make money off your investment decisions and transactions. You're better off working with fee-only RIAs. You can find these advisers through the National Association of Professional Advisers, and through referrals. Another resource for locating fee-only advisers is Dimensional Fund Advisors (www.dfaus.com), whose advisers can place assets in the funds it manages.

Don't make the mistake of thinking that your friends and associates are going to give you referrals to competent, conflict-free advisers. Unless they are very knowledgeable, they will usually tell you

> **mint hint**
>
> See "How to Find a Financial Advisor You Can Trust" by Ana Gonzalez Ribeiro (www.mint.com/blog/goals/what-to-look-for-in-a-financial-advisor) and related comments and videos for more perspectives on finding an adviser.

whether they like their adviser and impart a few anecdotal instances of good or bad advice.

What's the Point?

If you decide to retain an investment adviser, you should only use fee-only Registered Investment Advisors who will focus on your asset allocation and limit your investments to index funds, passively managed funds, or exchange traded funds.

PART SEVEN

Don't Fight the Markets

By investing in a globally diversified portfolio of low management fee stock and bond index funds, you can easily capture market returns. This part of the book tells you how.

CHAPTER 25

Don't Just Do Something— Stand There

In an efficient market, competition . . . leads to a situation where at any point in time, actual prices of individual securities already reflect the effects of information based both on events that have already occurred and on events which, as of now, the market expects to take place in the future. In other words, in an efficient market at any point in time the actual price of a security will be a good estimate of its intrinsic value.

—Eugene F. Fama, mathematician and author

In the 1950s, one of the big food companies introduced a cake mix for busy housewives. All they had to do was pour the mix into a bowl, add milk, beat the batter, pour it into a pan, and bake the cake. In marketing surveys housewives had said they didn't have time to deal with all the ingredients and steps required to bake a cake from scratch. However, they didn't enjoy using this new product.

The reason?

It didn't let them feel they were doing enough for their families. Baking expresses hands-on, I-took-the-trouble caring, and the mix wasn't allowing them to feel that way. This presented a problem, which the company solved neatly. They omitted the powdered egg from the mix and changed the directions to include the step "Add one egg" along with the two cups of milk. Adding the egg let the homemakers feel they were actually baking.

Like those homemakers, many investors want to *do something*. They want to buy low and sell high. They want to find hot stocks and new funds. They want to boost their returns to new, market-beating highs.

They would be better off investing in a globally diversified portfolio of low management fee index funds and avoiding the fees, taxes, and losses that hyperactive investors incur.

Let the Market Do the Work

Markets work amazingly well to resolve the forces of supply and demand through the price mechanism. We see this every day at the grocery store. Beef costs more than chicken. Lobster costs more than bluefish. People want more beef to grill this summer? Price goes up. Big lobster catch this season? Price goes down. We see the price mechanism in the supermarkets, housing markets, and labor markets. We not only live with it, we deeply believe in it.

Why do we jettison that belief when it comes to the stock and bond markets?

Given the quality and quantity of information on stocks and bonds and the speed at which that information is disseminated, it's simply irrational to think that stock prices are inaccurate, unfair, or outdated. Yet investors who readily pay the asking price for chicken, beef, and seafood search long and hard for stocks that are undervalued or overvalued—and then buy or sell hundreds or thousands of shares based on that belief.

Active fund managers and brokers and others who profit from having assets under management and doing transactions want investors to believe they—the fund managers, the investors, or both—are smarter than the market.

Can they value stocks more accurately than the millions of buyers and sellers in the capital markets? Can they (legally) obtain data, ferret out facts, or gain "insights" that will enable them to produce extraordinary returns? Do they really have a system, model, or set of analytics that can outsmart the market? Does their assessment of management's capabilities or the company's competitiveness somehow give them an edge over all other investors? Can their returns consistently outweigh the fees and costs of their attempts to beat the market?

The answer to all of these questions is no. No rational case has been made for active fund management. The returns of actively managed funds rarely outperform their designated market indexes over the long term. When they do, it is simply luck at work. No one has demonstrated the skill to beat the markets with any consistency.

Stop Caring So Much

It takes discipline to do nothing. Even nonhyperactive investors feel the need to fiddle with their investments. Why? Because they care. They want to be involved. They want to do something.

But you have to care enough to rein in your impulses, exercise discipline, and let the market do its job, which it will, as I explain in the next two chapters.

What's the Point?

The securities markets price securities effectively, efficiently, and accurately. There is no compelling case for active fund management.

CHAPTER 26

May the (Market) Force Be with You

Past performance is no guarantee of future performance.
—Disclaimer found in fund prospectuses

Most people laugh off the scam emails from Nigeria, where a lot of folks seem to need money to help them withdraw the large sums they have in that nation's banks. Most people also ignore emails from Britain telling them they just need to pay a few fees so they can collect their sweepstakes winnings.

Yet many of these same people take the prospect of outsized returns on investments very seriously. They carefully read faxes pitching penny stocks or prospectuses from hedge funds founded by former "stars" of Wall Street.

On a larger scale, millions of investors actually invest in actively managed funds. As Allan Roth, author of *How a Second Grader Beats Wall Street*, noted, popular sales tactics of these funds' managers include:

Outlandish promises: Promises of high returns are the favored bait. For example, a radio ad promised a *guaranteed* 8% return, compounded annually. Yet why would a fund delivering such returns need to advertise? Wouldn't institutional money flow to them without radio ads? Remember this: High returns always involve increased risk.

Death by disclosure: Make no mistake, a 200-page prospectus is designed to leave you completely confused. This trick was developed by trial lawyers, who during the disclosure process deliver a truckload of documents to the opposition and let them try to figure it out. Clarity is the last thing you'll find in most prospectuses. The primary purpose of these documents is to protect the companies issuing stock from lawsuits by investors. If they are sued for misrepresenting the risk of an investment, they can point to the small print in the prospectus and say: "What's your complaint? That risk was fully disclosed and you invested with full knowledge of it."

Cherry-picked benchmarks: A manager can say her fund earned 14% when the S&P 500 earned only 12.5%, and claim she beat the market. But the S&P 500 includes only the 500 largest U. S. stocks and omits dividends. The 2010 return on the *total* U. S. stock market was 17.7%. So that fund manager *underperformed* the broader market. It is very common for mutual funds to compare their returns to the wrong benchmark. Here's the key statistic you need to know: Less than 5% of actively managed funds beat their benchmarks over a 10-year period. The ones that did beat their benchmarks last year or the last 5 or 10 years often do not beat them over the corresponding future period.

Neither active fund managers nor stock pickers—nor you—can beat the market with any consistency, for three reasons:

Securities markets are efficient. As explained in Chapter 25, with few exceptions stocks and bonds are appropriately priced due to the efficiency of the markets. Trying to pick underval-ued stocks that will significantly appreciate is close to impos-sible, even for highly trained analysts who do it for a living.

Nobody can time the market. The markets are cyclical but unpredictable. A huge range of events can drive investors into or out of various asset classes. But those events and their effects are random and unpredictable (though it seems so obvious *after* the fact). Peaks and troughs in security and fund prices—and market movements in general—are impossible to forecast and act upon profitably.

Costs and fees reduce your returns. What I call hyperactive investing—ongoing efforts to improve investment perfor-mance by buying and selling securities or actively managed funds—boosts transaction costs and taxes. The costs are buried in management fees (also called *expense ratios*), which compensate the fund manager. If you trade on your own, you incur the fees directly. Unless the assets are in a tax-deferred account, you also pay taxes on realized gains.

mint hint

For additional perspectives on investing in index funds, see the *MintLife* blog posts tagged "index funds" (www.mint.com/blog/tag/index-funds).

Here's the bottom line: Stock picking, market timing, and investing in actively managed mutual funds benefit brokers who tout them. Investors should avoid them.

What's the Point?

The market will work for you, if you don't chase outsized returns and instead use only low management fee stock and bond index funds.

CHAPTER 27

Why Index Funds Work
for Investors

Active managers argue that less efficient markets provide the
opportunity for outperformance by skillful managers. However,
it's important to realize that a majority of active managers in a
given market will underperform the appropriate benchmark in the
long run whether markets are or are not efficient.

—Gary Karz, certified financial analyst

D
o you have the discipline to do nothing? Can you let the
market build wealth for you? Do you accept that active
managers' are likely to underperform their benchmarks?
Would you rather keep the money those managers take in fees?

If you answered yes to these questions, you are ready to learn
more about index funds. If you answered no you are ready to learn
more. Once you understand the benefits of low management fee
index funds, it's the only way you'll invest to build long-term wealth.

What Are Index Funds?

An index fund is a mutual fund made up of the securities in the
index in the proportions the index uses. An index is just a statis-

tical measure of an economic or financial change, usually from some base year. For example, the consumer price index measures inflation based on the price of a sample set of goods and services in a base year.

The most famous stock market indexes are the Dow Jones Industrial Average (DJIA) and the Standard & Poor's 500 (S&P 500). The DJIA is based on the stock prices of only 30 major companies. The S&P 500, which includes 500 companies, is a broader measure of the market. The Wilshire 5000 Total Market Index is the broadest index for the U.S. stock market. It measures the performance of all U.S. securities with readily available price data.

Indexes are compiled by financial information companies (like Standard & Poor's and Dow Jones), securities exchanges, and fund families (such as Vanguard and TIAA-CREF). The securities in many indexes are chosen for specific characteristics, such as type of security (stock or bond funds, etc.), company size in terms of capitalization (large-, mid-, or small-cap funds), industry (technology, energy, retail, etc.), or location (Europe, Asia, emerging markets, etc.). An index can combine characteristics, such as European mid-cap stocks, or include all stocks traded on an exchange, such as the New York Stock Exchange.

An index fund includes all (or almost all) of the securities in the index, in the proportions that the index includes them. The returns earned by the index fund reflect the collective returns that the securities in the index earn, less the costs incurred by the index fund.

What's Great About Index Funds?

Here are the main advantages of investing in index funds:

Diversification: Diversification spreads risks across many securities so those that do well offset those that do poorly. A fund that benchmarks the total U.S. stock market offers broad diversification, but adding an international fund that consists of stocks of foreign companies offers additional diversification. I recommend allocating your investments across several funds to meet your need for returns and your tolerance for risk, as I discuss in Chapter 28.

Low management fees: Index fund management fees are low because the fund manager buys and sells securities only to match the composition of the index, which changes when the index adds or drops companies. Index fund managers are paid less than active managers because they follow this recipe and thus have less work to do. Active fund managers research, buy, and sell securities to try to beat a designated market benchmark (the index). They usually fail to do so. However, index fund fees vary, so you must seek out *low management fee* index funds, as I discuss in Part Eight.

Predictable risk: The risks associated with the returns on index funds are lower than those of individual securities due to diversification. Those risks are more predictable because the return on an investment in a large number of companies is more predictable than the returns on individual companies or small numbers of companies.

Ease of purchase: Investment companies make it easy to set up an account and to buy shares in index funds. They offer online information on the funds and their composition, goals, risks, and historical returns and provide monthly or quarterly statements on performance.

Choice: While you can buy a broad-based index fund like one that benchmarks the Wilshire 5000, you can also buy more focused funds. There are hundreds of index funds to choose from, including many that have been around for decades. As explained in Part Eight, I recommend that you assemble a portfolio of funds to meet your investment goals subject to the level of risk you can accept. You can put together a very intelligent portfolio with only three index funds. While the securities industry likes to make investing appear to be terribly complex, it's actually quite simple.

Index funds are the smartest, easiest, lowest stress way for individual investors—and institutions—to invest. Yet many people still resist investing this way.

But . . . But . . . But . . .

Here are the three most common arguments I hear against index based investing:

My cousin (friend/boss/in-law) bought a stock and it doubled/tripled/quadrupled in x months. Why shouldn't I do that too?

Because it's not a consistent, reliable, low-risk investment strategy for building long-term wealth. For every stock like that, many more produce poor returns because people can rarely time a peak or trough in a stock's price. It also generates losses and costs that are rarely mentioned in these tales of investing prowess. Just like in Las Vegas, some gamblers hit the jackpot, but most go home losers.

What if I see huge returns in part of the market and feel that I'm missing out?

Take comfort in knowing that you will miss the lows (and losses) as well as the highs (and gains), and that neither can be predicted. Find your excitement elsewhere. Or, strictly as a hobby, put a very small portion of your portfolio into investments like initial public offerings, gold, or hot stocks. You will probably incur losses, but it could satisfy your need to gamble with your money.

What if the markets are in a down cycle when I want to take my money out?

This is a concern to address in your asset allocation and retirement planning. In general, if you need cash during a down cycle, you can

> ### mint hint
>
> Go to the source of much of modern investment wisdom by reading the Mint.com interview "A Random Walk Talk with Burton Malkiel" (www.mint.com/blog/investing/mint-qa-a-random-walk-talk-with-burton-malkiel). Burton Malkiel is the author of the classic book on investing *A Random Walk Down Wall Street*.

selectively liquidate specific portions of your portfolio (like bonds), borrow against certain assets, or draw against a whole life policy. Borrowing from a life insurance policy can have serious adverse consequences, so you should do so only after exhausting other possibilities and after seeking appropriate advice. If you are retired or need ready access to cash for other reasons, you can also use money market funds or certain certificates of deposit.

What's the Point?

Index funds track the performance of the securities in a designated index. By capturing the returns of the global marketplace, your returns will exceed those of the majority of actively managed portfolios.

CHAPTER 28

The Risk-Return Tradeoff

The first step in the risk management process is to acknowledge
the reality of risk. Denial is a common tactic that substitutes
deliberate ignorance for thoughtful planning.
—Charles Tremper, director, Strategic Planning and Partner Relations
Center for Digital Innovation, University of California at Los Angeles

nvesting is risky, especially when you consider the various
types of risks you face:

- **Credit risk:** The company you're invested in may be unable
  to pay its obligations.

- **Inflation risk:** Inflation may erode your returns or asset
  values.

- **Interest rate risk:** Bond prices may decline due to rising
  rates.

- **Foreign exchange risk:** Currency movements may erode
  your returns.

- **Liquidity risk:** You might not be able to sell an asset due to
  market conditions.

- **Risk of principal:** You could lose some or all of the amount you've invested.

- **Market risk:** You cannot diversify away all the volatility of an asset class.

You have to understand—and live with—risk if you're going to be an investor.

Financial managers and investment bankers have ways of managing these risks. Some methods work better than others, but none is perfect.

Most individual investors place bets rather than manage risk. Others are so averse to risk—particularly risk of principal—that they don't invest or are too conservative with their investments. They keep their money in bank accounts or U.S. bonds. However, they still incur inflation risk, while passing up the higher returns available in stock and corporate bond funds. If inflation exceeds the rate of return of these "conservative" investments, the combination of inflation and taxes makes this conservative strategy very risky.

Smart investing begins with understanding the relationship between risks and returns.

How Much Risk to Take

Smart investing is taking fairly predictable risks in anticipation of fairly predictable returns. The primary determinate of risk is how much of your portfolio is invested in stocks and how much is invested in bonds. The higher the exposure to stocks, the higher the risk.

More precise measures of risk are slightly more complex. The basic measure of risk is standard deviation, which measures the volatility of a stock, bond, or portfolio. Standard deviation measures the dispersion of returns—their deviation from the average return for the asset class. The higher the standard deviation, the greater the dispersion, volatility, and risk of an asset or asset class.

Conservative investments like U.S. Treasury bonds pay relatively low returns and have low standard deviations. More aggressive investments, like large company stocks, pay higher returns and have higher standard deviations. Small company stocks pay even higher returns and have even higher standard deviations.

Conservative investors should target an overall maximum standard deviation of 8% in their portfolios, moderately aggressive investors a maximum of 15%, and very aggressive investors, a maximum of 20%. No one's portfolio should have a standard deviation above 30%.

You can find the standard deviation of a fund in its prospectus or at its website. Your broker is unlikely to understand standard deviation, much less calculate the risk of your portfolio. His or her concern is often focused on returns, often without regard to risk. Yet another reason to avoid brokers.

How Much Risk for How Much Return?

In general, riskier investments pay higher returns because investors require higher returns in exchange for accepting higher risk. From the investor's perspective, the risks stem from three main factors:

- **Market:** Stocks have higher expected returns than bonds; foreign markets have higher returns than domestic markets.

- **Size:** Small companies' stocks have higher expected returns than large companies'.

- **Price:** "Value stocks" have higher expected returns than "growth stocks."

The goal in constructing a portfolio is to combine asset classes that have different levels of risk to attain a targeted return (asset price appreciation, and dividends and interest) for a specific overall, acceptable level of risk (as measured by standard deviation). Your portfolio should be constructed from various asset classes on the basis of past growth, returns, and risk.

Keep these factors in mind:

- **Risk and return are generally positively correlated:** The higher the return, the higher the risk. The conservative portfolio is less risky, but provides lower returns.

- **Risk diminishes over time:** Across each portfolio, the standard deviation tends to decrease as the investment period lengthens.

- **Compounding is extremely powerful:** Look at historical returns over long periods of time, preferably 20 years or more.

How Much Risk Is Right for You?

How much risk to incur depends on your age, financial goals, and tolerance for risk. Once you decide, you can allocate your money across a portfolio of low-cost index funds that reflects your desired risk-return tradeoff. That portfolio will balance risks against returns so that, over the long term, you earn a fair return for the risks you accept.

The following allocations illustrate this concept:

	Equities	Bonds
Low risk	20%	80%
Medium-low risk	40%	60%
Medium risk	60%	40%
Medium-high risk	80%	20%
High risk	100%	0%

 mint hint

At Mint.com, you can find videos on investing, such as Roger Grow of Grow Asset Management in "Where Is the Best Place to Invest Your Money?" (https://www.mint.com/invest/where-is-the-best-place-to-invest-your-money). Also, Mint's "Ways to Invest" section provides users with advice on the right tools for their investment style (https://wwws.mint.com/investment.event).

These broad allocations don't indicate which stock or bond funds to invest in. I'm only illustrating that bonds are more conservative (lower risk and return) than stocks, and stocks are more aggressive (higher risk and return) than bonds. How you allocate your investments between stocks and bonds is the primary determinant of the amount of risk you will be taking.

What's the Point?

A cardinal rule of investing is that the tradeoff for higher returns is higher risk.

PART EIGHT

Putting Your Money to Work

When you start investing you won't be looking for thrills and excitement from your portfolio. Instead, you'll be seeking the satisfaction that comes with knowing your money is working for you instead of for others. As the years go by, you'll find that watching your wealth steadily grow can be a very good feeling.

In this part, you will learn how to assess your risk capacity, minimize costs, understand asset allocation, open an account, and start investing.

CHAPTER 29

Assessing Your Risk Capacity

It is clear from both everyday and clinical observation that people
differ widely in their attitude toward risk, some being frightened
of the slightest exposure while others seem actively to seek out
risky situations.

—John Steiner, British psychoanalyst

In May 2008, Manhattan doorman Richie Randazzo won a $5
million jackpot in a daily scratch-off game called Set for Life.
He spends about $30 a week on lottery tickets. Ray Otero, a
superintendent in a nearby building, found the aptly named
Richie's good fortune hard to accept. "When I heard he won, I
got so mad. I spend all that money and [Richie] wins," he told the
New York Times. "It's wrong."

Ray spends $500 to $700 a week on lottery tickets—a total of
$30,000 in 2007 alone. (Ray's take-home pay is about $40,000 a
year, net of a free apartment, odd jobs, and tips.)

You don't need to be Warren Buffett to appreciate how preferable it would have been for Ray to put his $500 to $700 a week into
index funds. Yet, while Ray Otero may not be happy with his lack
of returns on his lottery "investments," he may enjoy taking risks.

Investors who see Ray's approach as different from their own might consider their attitudes toward risk—especially if they are hyperactive investors. These folks chase outsized returns by trying to time the peaks and valleys of the stock market. They get into day trading, and buy gold or other investments featured in the financial news depending on what's hot at the moment.

Their behavior, motivation, and even brain chemistry closely resemble those of casino gamblers. According to Jason Zweig, "Delving into the brain with MRI and other scanning techniques, scientists can now observe the mechanisms our brains use to reckon the value of rewards, interpret probabilities and estimate risks—the very essence of investing." Zweig's studies confirm that active investors (those who attempt to beat the markets) experience the release of dopamine when presented with the opportunity of a surging stock. Brain imaging shows that the neural circuits stimulated by the prospect of big profits are identical to those that lead to drug, gambling, and alcohol addiction.

You need to take a more rational approach to risk if you want to be a successful investor.

Approaching Risk Rationally

As I explained in Part Seven, investing involves gauging risks and returns, deciding what your risk capacity is, and *then* deciding where to invest.

Here are five major factors to consider as you assess your risk capacity:

Time horizon and liquidity needs: The longer your time horizon and the further into the future you can push your need for liquidity, the greater your risk capacity. If you don't need to withdraw 20% or more of your money for 10 years or more (preferably 15 or 20), you can weather market cycles and choose higher return asset classes. If the time horizon of your investment is less than 5 years, you should have *zero* exposure to the stock market.

Income and savings rate: The higher your income and savings rate, the greater your risk capacity. Your risk capacity decreases if you have a high-income but a high-cost lifestyle and low savings rate. It increases if you spend less than you make and save more (at least 10% of your income). Your risk capacity also increases with your level of investment income.

Net worth: The higher your net worth, the greater your risk capacity because you have a buffer against short-term market volatility. As you know from Chapter 5, high net worth results from high assets and low liabilities. The more assets you can tap in a time of need and the lower your liabilities, the higher your risk capacity.

Attitude toward risk: How do you feel about losing money? No one likes it, but if you can emotionally tolerate losses in the current value of your portfolio, your risk capacity rises. This is what most people think of as risk tolerance. If you can maintain your peace of mind during a 50% loss in value, you have a high tolerance for risk. If a 20% loss causes you sleepless nights, you are fairly risk averse.

Investment knowledge: I don't mean knowledge of stock picking, day trading, and stock options. I mean knowledge of modern portfolio theory and of the risk-return profile of your current and potential investments. If you're not knowledgeable, I've recommended sources in the notes to this chapter (see Part Twelve). In general, the greater your investment knowledge, the higher your capacity for risk.

I strongly recommend that you take the Risk Capacity Survey at my website (smartestinvestmentbook.com). This survey will give you an initial assessment of your risk capacity and knowledge of what goes into it.

Use the factors I've mentioned in this chapter *and* the Risk Capacity Survey *and* your self-knowledge to characterize your risk capacity so you can choose a portfolio that is suitable for you.

Don't Roll the Dice

Knowing your risk capacity permits you to choose investments that will maximize your returns given the risk you can assume. You can learn how to increase or decrease your risk capacity by adjusting the factors I described.

For example, you can increase your risk capacity by:

- Increasing your time horizon or decreasing your liquidity needs (or both).

- Increasing your income or your savings rate (or both).

- Increasing your net worth by increasing assets or decreasing liabilities.

- Learning to tolerate more risk in exchange for potentially higher returns.

- Learning about portfolio theory and risk, returns, and asset allocation.

> ### 🌿 mint hint
>
> For additional perspectives on investing risk, see "Investing 101: Defining Your Risk Tolerance" by Michael C. Thomsett (http://mint.com/blog/investing/investing-101-risk-tolerance-09282010).

Most investors react emotionally to short-term market movements that temporarily increase or decrease asset values. Approaching risk rationally helps you avoid those reactions to market volatility and saves you time, money, and headaches.

What's the Point?

You can invest more effectively if you understand the factors that determine your risk capacity: time, income, net worth, attitude toward risk, and knowledge.

CHAPTER 30

Fighting the Worst Enemies of High Returns

The miracle of compounding returns is overwhelmed by the tyranny of compounding costs.

—John C. Bogle, founder of the Vanguard Group, and author of
The Little Book of Common Sense Investing

Picture your investments as a huge trough where hungry hogs are permitted, and even encouraged, to slurp up part of your returns. These hogs take the form of brokers, active fund managers, anyone who encourages active trading, most 401(k) plan advisers, and tax authorities. They do this through high fees, expenses, taxes, incompetence, and other, often hidden, costs.

All of these are enemies of your wealth. An investment of $50,000 at 8% would grow to about $342,000 in 25 years. Lower that annual return by just 2% and your nest egg shrinks to about $215,000. Actively managed funds, and 401(k) and similar plans, set you up to fatten these hogs, and you'll see few slices of bacon in return. As you now know, the key defense against these enemies is investing in low management fee index funds—to which I add the following guidelines.

Avoid House Funds

Most brokerage firms have sponsored or assembled funds with their own names, such as the Merrill Lynch Aggressive Growth Fund. Only the firm's brokers can sell a house fund, and they do sell them because they're paid higher commissions on them. There's no evidence that these funds outperform either the market or funds from independent fund families. Indeed a 10-year study showed they underperformed the latter.

Be Sure It's Managed as a True Index Fund

Any fund can drift from its stated investment strategy and objectives. In fact, a study of Morningstar's database for 1993 to 1996 found that 54% of mutual funds drifted from their stated style. Drift is less likely with an index fund because the fund manager only has to track the index. But even an index fund manager might increase the cash equivalents held by the fund. In that case, a fund can experience cash drag—failure to match the return on the index (more broadly known as performance drag).

Avoid Funds with Classes of Shares

Mutual funds with Class A, B, and C shares are designed to extract commissions from investors. On Class A shares investors pay a commission (or load) when they buy the shares (front-end load). On Class B shares they pay a commission when they sell the shares (back-end load). This commission declines the longer the shares are held. Class C shares resemble Class B except the commission *rises* over time (to encourage more selling and buying!). Salespeople push the products with the highest commissions, and all of these products reduce your returns. Index funds do not have multiple share classes.

Minimize Costs

- Compare the expense ratios of any funds you are considering. The expense ratio is the amount that mutual fund shareholders pay for operating expenses and management fees, as a percentage of the total invested in the fund. Index funds have far lower expense ratios than actively managed funds.

- With any mutual fund be particularly careful of these devils:
  - *12-B-1 fee:* Named for a section of the Investment Company Act of 1940, this is an annual marketing or distribution fee, ranging from 0.25% to 1% (the maximum permitted), paid on a mutual fund. Originally designed to lower expenses by growing the size of the fund, the fee has in fact raised costs to the investor.
  - *Wrap fees:* Instead of commissions on fund or stock purchases, the firm charges 2% to 3% of the portfolio's value as a wrap fee. Wrap accounts are usually managed by outside fund managers who receive a share of the fee. The investment company does less work while the fund manager typically fails to beat market returns.
  - *Trading costs:* The costs of trades are not included in the expense ratio. The more transactions an active fund does, the higher the trading costs. Actively managed funds typically have higher trading costs than index funds.

Minimize Taxes

Many investors instinctively gravitate to a tax-deferred account—like a 401(k) plan or a traditional individual retirement account (IRA). With these plans, you incur no tax liability until you withdraw funds.

However, the actual tax effects will depend on the marginal tax rate when you withdraw the money. You may be at the risk of *higher* taxes if you put too much money in tax-deferred accounts and forgo the lower capital gains tax rates. When investing, it's essential to consider not only your desire or need for current income tax deductions, but also the tax efficiency of your long-term investments.

Index funds are among the most tax-efficient investments you will find. Index funds do fewer transactions, which minimizes capital gains and capital gains taxes. The pre-tax and after-tax performances of index funds are therefore very similar. From the tax perspective, index funds' low activity generally results in such low taxation that it is almost equivalent to putting your money into an IRA. In fact, in can be better because on withdrawal your investment and gains will be taxed at the capital gains tax rate rather than the higher income tax rate.

From a tax-efficiency standpoint, consider a portfolio of index funds. I provide specific recommendations in Chapter 32.

Understand Your 401(k) or 403(b) or 457 Plan

As I explained in *The Smartest 401(k) Book You'll Ever Read*, 401(k) and related plans are "giant skimming operations, where brokers and mutual funds act in concert with employers to deprive employees of market returns." I discuss how this occurs and what to do about it in Chapter 34.

> **mint hint**
>
> See Maria O'Brien's "How to Invest for Less" for additional information on investment fees and how to avoid them (http://mint.com/blog/finance-core/how-to-invest-for-less).

What's the Point?

The enemies of high returns are high fees, costs, and taxes.

CHAPTER 31

The Simple Logic of Asset Allocation

Over the [past] 35 years, American business has delivered terrific results. It should therefore have been easy for investors to earn juicy returns: All they had to do was piggyback Corporate America in a diversified, low-expense way. An index fund that they never touched would have done the job. Instead many investors have had experiences ranging from mediocre to disastrous.

—*Berkshire Hathaway Annual Report*, 2004

Asset class allocation is *the* key factor affecting your returns. Studies have shown that asset allocation accounts for 90% to 100% of the variance in performance of a portfolio over time. The variance measures the dispersion of returns compared with an average for the stock, bond, or portfolio, so it's a measure of the risk associated with those returns. The standard deviation, discussed in Chapter 28, is the most common measure of variance, or risk, used in investing.

Asset allocation refers to the division of an investment portfolio among three types of investments—stocks, bonds, and cash equivalents (such as certificates of deposit and money market funds). The percentages allocated to these broad asset classes enable you to choose the risk-return profile of your investments. These percentages account for far, far more of a portfolio's performance than the specific securities in it. In fact, the specific securities account for only 5% of the variance in a portfolio's returns.

This fact reinforces the case for index funds compared to stock picking and active management of a long-term investment portfolio. Why spend time on an activity that accounts for only 5% of the variance in returns, especially when it depends on luck rather than skill?

Asset allocation is a lot simpler, and far more effective.

Asset Allocation Demystified

There are formulas for asset allocation, but most are too simplistic. One is to subtract your age from 100 and use the answer as the percentage of your portfolio to allocate to stocks. Thus a 20-year-old would allocate 80% to stocks, a 30-year-old 70%, and so on. The remaining percentage would go into bonds.

This formula omits factors other than age, but it's better than just putting 80%, 90%, or 100% into stocks, which is what many hyperactive investors do. Even this simple formula recognizes that as you age and approach the need for investment income your risk capacity decreases.

Generally, there are four major factors to consider in determining your asset allocation:

- Your age (and health).
- Your savings.
- Your need for retirement income.
- Your risk capacity.

Here are what the key asset allocation factors mean:

- The younger you are and the better your health, the more of your portfolio you can allocate to stock funds.

- The higher your ratio of retirement savings to retirement living expenses, the more of your portfolio you can allocate to stock funds.

- The higher your retirement plan contributions and salary growth, the more you can allocate to stock funds.

- The higher your capacity for risk, the more you can allocate to stock funds.

About 70% of the percentage of your portfolio you invest in low-cost stock index funds should be in U.S. stock index funds and 30% in international stock index funds. The percentage not invested in stock index funds should be in bond index funds.

Index Funds Are Ideal for Investors

I believe all investors should purchase *only* index funds for their investment portfolios. Here's my reasoning:

- **You know what you are buying:** An index fund tracks a designated benchmark (like the Wilshire 5000), so there's no guesswork about what's in that part of your portfolio.

- **You can better gauge risks and returns:** An index fund manager matches the fund's holdings to the index, so you don't have the uncertainties created by active managers' often futile efforts to boost returns.

- **You can more easily rebalance:** Because you can better gauge risks and returns, you can change your allocations more accurately with index funds than with actively managed funds.

As with any investment, past risks and returns of index funds may not be those of the future. However, a globally diversified portfolio of low management fee stock and bond index funds (in an asset allocation suitable for you) is likely to generate returns significantly higher than a comparable portfolio of actively managed funds over the long term.

What "They" Say and What to Do

They say invest in stocks when you're young, and that's good advice. But don't invest in individual stocks or actively managed stock funds. The returns will rarely beat the index and fees will erode your returns.

They say invest in technology, healthcare, or other hot stocks or funds. Do that, and you'll try to pick stocks and funds and wind up with more investments than you can track *and* lower returns. I recommend investing in three low management fee index funds from reputable fund families.

> **mint hint**
>
> See "The Lazy Portfolio: Asset Allocation Made Easy" by Peter McKie (http://mint.com/blog/investing/asset-allocation-08232010) for several sound approaches to building a solid portfolio.

They say bonds are for old folks who need low-risk and regular income. That makes sense, but many young and not-so-young investors take this to mean avoid bonds. That's bad advice. Low management fee bond index funds help you manage risk. Good bond funds can offset the risk of more aggressive investments.

No matter what they say, you should accept enough risk to obtain returns that meet your goals while providing enough safety so you don't sustain major long-term losses.

What's the Point?

Switch your focus from market timing and stock picking to asset allocation. Implement your asset allocation with low management fee index funds.

CHAPTER 32

A Simple Way to Implement Your Investing Plan

Market timing is a poor substitute for a long-term investment plan.
—Jonathan Clements, personal finance journalist

Now that you've assessed your risk capacity, learned about enemies of returns, and determined your asset allocation, you're ready to start investing. To do this you simply:

- Open an account with a fund family.

- Invest in the index funds that are right for you.

- Rebalance your portfolio periodically.

Step 1. Open an Account with a Fund Family

Fund families subject you to minimal sales pressure, have an excellent selection of low management fee index funds, and are easy to do business with, online or on the phone.

The fund families I recommend are Vanguard Group, Fidelity

Investments, and T. Rowe Price—none of which I am affiliated with in any way. You might consider using others like Charles Schwab & Co. (www.schwab.com). Just be sure that the fund family you choose offers a low management fee index fund that benchmarks the stocks actively traded in the United States, an international stock index fund, and a U.S. bond index fund. I provide the names and symbols of the index funds I recommend below, so you don't need to be concerned about which fund you should select.

Fidelity and Vanguard are among the largest and best-known fund families, and their fees on funds of the type I recommend are among the lowest. While smaller, T. Rowe Price is also a no-load fund family with significant assets under management. Here is the basic contact information for each:

Fidelity Investments
www.fidelity.com
800-343-3548

Vanguard Group
www.vanguard.com
877-662-7447

T. Rowe Price
www.troweprice.com
800-638-5660

The websites of these firms offer plentiful information and enable you to open a new account, transfer money into your account, and buy the funds you want.

Step 2. Invest in the Index Funds That Are Right for You

To make it as easy as possible to invest in the right funds, the tables in this section tell you which funds to select and what percentage of your stock and bond allocation to invest in each one, given your risk capacity (discussed in Chapter 29). Your risk capacity will translate to a preference for a low-risk, medium-low-risk, medium-risk, medium-high-risk, or high-risk portfolio.

The percentages in the tables refer to the percentages of the *total amount invested in the portfolio* (that is, the total sum invested in the three funds). In each case, 70% of the *amount invested in stocks* is in a U.S. stock index fund and 30% of the *amount invested in stocks* is in an international stock index fund. The remaining 30% of the total portfolio is in the bond fund. (You

VANGUARD MODEL PORTFOLIOS

Fund Name	Low Risk	Medium-Low Risk	Medium Risk	Medium-High Risk	High Risk
Total Stock Market Index Fund (VTSMX)	14%	28%	42%	56%	70%
Total International Stock Index Fund (VGTSX)	6%	12%	18%	24%	30%
Total Bond Market Index Fund (VBMFX)	80%	60%	40%	20%	0%
	100%	100%	100%	100%	100%

FIDELITY MODEL PORTFOLIOS

Fund Name	Low Risk	Medium-Low Risk	Medium Risk	Medium-High Risk	High Risk
Fidelity Spartan Total Market Index Fund (FSTMX)	14%	28%	42%	56%	70%
Fidelity Spartan International Index Fund (FSIIX)	6%	12%	18%	24%	30%
Fidelity Spartan U.S. Bond Index Fund (FBIDX)	80%	60%	40%	20%	0%
	100%	100%	100%	100%	100%

T. ROWE PRICE MODEL PORTFOLIOS

Fund Name	Low Risk	Medium-Low Risk	Medium Risk	Medium-High Risk	High Risk
T. Rowe Price Total Equity Market Fund (POMIX)	14%	28%	42%	56%	70%
T. Rowe Price International Equity Index Fund (PIEQX)	6%	12%	18%	24%	30%
T. Rowe Price U.S. Bond Index Fund (PBDIX)	80%	60%	40%	20%	0%
	100%	100%	100%	100%	100%

will find long-term [20-year] risk and return data for these portfolios in the appendix.)

A few caveats:

- If you have less than a total of $25,000 to invest, you may not be able to use these allocations because of the minimum investment requirements of some funds. In that case you'll have to adjust your allocations—for example, by forgoing the international fund. Then when your portfolio is large enough, you can use the optimum allocations.

- If you invest with another fund family, you may have to invest in four funds because there may be no total market index fund. If so, in the fund family you choose, put 60% of your stock allocation into the S&P 500 index fund; put 10% of your stock allocation into the U.S. small stock index fund; put 30% of your stock allocation into the international equity index fund; and put 100% of your bond allocation into the U. S. bond index fund.

- You can also invest this way using exchange traded funds (EFTs). ETFs may be an option if you don't meet the minimum investment thresholds, since ETFs typically don't have a minimum investment requirement.

In *The Smartest Portfolio You'll Ever Own*, I recommend additional index based portfolios, including a portfolio that tilts toward small and value stocks. There is considerable research indicating portfolios structured in this manner yield higher returns for a given level of risk.

Step 3. Rebalance Your Portfolio Periodically

The allocations in your portfolio will change as the values of shares in the funds increase or decrease. For example, your 70:30 stock-to-bond ratio may over time move to 85:15 due to rising stock prices. Since asset allocation determines your risk and return, when that happens you'll have to rebalance your portfolio. You may also have to rebalance if your need for investment income changes (for example, if you retire) or if your risk capacity changes.

There are three ways to rebalance your portfolio:

1. If you invest additional money in your portfolio, you can buy more of the assets that are underrepresented to achieve your desired allocation.

2. If you must work with your existing assets, you should sell the overrepresented ones and purchase the underrepresented ones to achieve your desired allocation.

3. If you work with an investment adviser, have him or her contact you every three to six months and review your portfolio. Also, contact your adviser if your situation changes. You can then discuss any need to rebalance, and your adviser can execute any necessary changes.

You can eliminate the need to rebalance by using a target retirement fund, which automatically rebalances your portfolio at regular intervals. Many fund families offer these funds. You pick a fund with a designated retirement date in its name (like the Vanguard Target Retirement 2035 Fund), and the fund automatically becomes more conservative over time, eliminating the need to change your asset allocation or to rebalance. I recommend the target retirement funds managed by Vanguard because all of the underlying funds are index funds and the management fees are very low.

---

mint hint

Mint.com's "Ways to Invest" tools (https://www.mint.com/waystoinvest) can help you to get started in investing, easily and quickly. Mint.com will also track your investment returns, performance versus benchmark index (like the S&P or Dow), and keep track of your cost basis under their "Investments" tab. Because Mint.com links to over 1,000 brokerages, your trades and portfolio will be accurately reflected without the need to manually enter ticker symbols, prices, or trades.

Investing Versus Saving, Revisited

As discussed in Part Two, you should keep a sum equal to three to six months (or more) of your monthly expenses in the bank. Don't put cash you may need in the short term into long-term investments. There are risks associated with investing that don't apply to savings, and you assume those risks to achieve higher returns.

What's the Point?

Investing in index funds with a fund family is very straightforward and so is periodically rebalancing your portfolio.

PART NINE

Real Retirement Planning

Whether you call it retirement or financial independence, you're always investing with that goal ultimately in mind. The more sharply you have defined it in dollars, the better your chances of reaching it. Most retirement planning is either too rudimentary or too reliant on 401(k) and similar plans, which serve the financial services industry rather than investors.

The following chapters will help you develop a plan that will work. It will also help you address the task of making your money last for the rest of your life.

CHAPTER 33

How Much Will You Need?

You can never be too rich or too thin.
—Wallis Simpson, Duchess of Windsor

How much income will you need to retire comfortably? Most experts say 75% of your preretirement income annually. That would mean saving 15% of your income *every year for 40 years.*

How much needs to be in your retirement portfolio? One common rule of thumb is 20 times your annual income while employed. If your income is $75,000, you'd need a portfolio of *$1.5 million.*

However you figure it, you need a goal. The Employee Benefits Research Institute notes that more than 50% of workers have not computed how much they'll need to retire. Your starting point for retirement planning should be the income you want to retire on.

But I Don't Plan on Retiring

You may plan on *not* retiring because you enjoy your work or see retirement as dull. If so, plan anyway. If you never need the money, your heirs and favorite charities will remember you fondly.

If you become unable to work due to accident, illness, infirmity, or career reversals, you will live with greater dignity and more options. Most disability income policies expire at age 65, and certain accidents or illnesses make work impossible. Do you want to spend your later years facing cancer, Alzheimer's, crippling arthritis, or the effects of a stroke *and* having to worry about money?

Factors to Consider

Suppose your household income is $80,000 a year (a bit above the hurdle for the top 25%, which was $77,500 in 2005, based on U.S. Census data). Around 75% of that is $60,000 a year or $5,000 a month before taxes. To earn that sum, you'd need a $1 million portfolio earning 6% a year, or a $750,000 portfolio earning 8%.

These calculations can be deceptive because:

- Returns can't be accurately predicted, particularly in retirement, and they are unlikely to be at the same level every year.

- You shouldn't withdraw all returns in a year, especially early in retirement.

- You'll probably have other income sources, such as Social Security, an annuity, or a pension, and you should count them too.

As you set your goal, take a close look at your expenses in retirement.

Consider Your Costs

Instead of living on 75% of your income, perhaps you can get that percentage down to 65%, or less.

Consider all the expenses that decrease or disappear at normal retirement age:

- Commuting and maybe one vehicle (many two-car couples downsize to one).

- Lunches and after-hours gatherings.

- Some clothing and dry cleaning bills.

- Mortgage payments *if* you have paid yours off.

- Life insurance (which may be paid up or, if term insurance, expired).

The more costs you drive down while maintaining a comfortable lifestyle, the better. With housing the largest expense for most people, paying your mortgage off is the best thing you can do. Property taxes can also be burdensome. In areas like Long Island and New Jersey, they can approach a thousand dollars a month for a three-bedroom house. If you're attracted to a lower tax area, it may be wise to move there. Also, downsizing to a smaller home can save thousands in heating, cooling, maintenance, *and* taxes.

Don't jettison your favorite pastimes. Sports, hobbies, culture, travel, and socializing keep you engaged with life and make retirement enjoyable.

Yet some costs *increase*, particularly healthcare. Be sure you understand your Medicare benefits, which cover 80% of most procedures. Seriously consider Medigap insurance to cover the difference. Long-term care insurance, which can be costly but can increase peace of mind and financial security, is also worth researching (see Chapter 39).

After you calculate your annual retirement income, you can

more accurately calculate the size of the portfolio you will need—and the amount you'll have to save.

Let's Do the Numbers

The following factors go into calculating the amount you will need to save to have the portfolio you will require:

- Your retirement age minus your current age.
- Current household income (including your spouse's).
- Current amount you have saved toward retirement (in all retirement accounts).
- Rate of return before retirement.
- Rate of return during retirement.
- Expected average annual rate of salary increases.
- Years of retirement income you believe you will need.
- Percent of income you'll need in retirement (based on the final year you worked).
- Expected average rate of inflation.

All of these factors contribute to determining how much you must save each year until you retire.

Fortunately, various online calculators account for these factors and calculate this number for you.

- **CNNMoney.com:** This planner analyzes your goals, income, savings, and portfolio to tell you whether you are on track (http://cgi.money.cnn.com/tools/retirementplanner/retire mentplanner.jsp).

- **ESPlanner:** This planner was created by Boston University economics professor Laurence Kotlikoff. Basic functions are free at the site, which charges about $60 for a more detailed version (https://basic.esplanner.com).

- **Index Funds Advisors (IFA):** The IFA has a free online calculator that considers multiple factors and helps you create your retirement plan (www .ifa.com/portfolios/Port ReturnCalc/index.aspx).

mint hint

See "An Upside-Down Approach to Retirement Planning" by Matthew Amster-Burton for a sound method of calculating your retirement income needs (www.mint.com/blog/goals/upside-investing-02082011).

- **Monte Carlo analysis:** I have one on my website that generates future return scenarios and computes the likelihood of your portfolio lasting through your retirement (www.smart estinvestmentbook.com).

Any of these calculators can produce goals that you may see as impossible to achieve. If that happens, your assumptions may be unrealistic and you'll have to adjust them until you have an achievable goal. This may involve boosting your income, cutting expenses so you can increase savings, lowering your retirement income needs, or taking greater risks in your asset allocations to achieve higher returns.

What's the Point?

If you actually calculate what you will need in retirement, you will be better able to plan your retirement.

CHAPTER 34

Beating the 401(k) Rip-Off

The [401(k)] plan fees are too high, or the fees are buried deep in disclosure documents where they are all but impossible to tally or are not revealed at all, or the providers are tainted by conflicts of interest or even de facto pay-for-play kickbacks.

—Neil Weinburg, financial journalist

Millions of people use 401(k) plans (and 403[b] and 457 plans as well) as their basic retirement account. However, most of these plans charge unconscionable fees that reduce participants' returns.

These plans are free to employers, but employees are being robbed because their returns are shared with a host of vendors who essentially pay to win the business. This occurs through a system of legal kickbacks.

The broker, in exchange for subsidizing the administrative costs of the plan, gets a monopoly from the employer on selecting the funds for the plan. The broker chooses funds based on payments *received from mutual funds who want to be included as investment options in the plan.* More than 90% of plan advisers (brokers and insurance companies) accept these kickbacks. If you've been wondering why your 401(k) returns have grown so slowly, this may be the reason. Congress has shown no interest in changing this system, but you *can* beat it.

Index funds typically will not pay kickbacks to be included as investment options in retirement plans. It's not surprising that the best investments for plan participants are either underrepresented or entirely missing from most of these plans.

Evaluate Your 401(k)

To evaluate your 401(k):

- **Review your plan.** Look for appropriate fund offerings, which should include:
  - A broad U.S. stock market *index* fund with a benchmark like the Wilshire 5000.
  - A broad international stock *index* fund with a benchmark like the MSCI AC World Index (excluding the United States).
  - A broad U.S. bond *index* fund with a benchmark like the Barclays Capital Aggregate Bond Index.
  - The option of a target retirement fund (aka Lifecycle Fund), but be sure expenses are reasonable and the underlying funds are index funds. These requirements currently limit acceptable choices to target retirement funds managed by Vanguard (vanguard.com).
  - Check to see if your 401(k) has a Roth option. If it does, and if you can afford to forgo the immediate tax deduction and to contribute after-tax dollars to your plan, do so. The income limitations on individual Roth IRAs don't apply to Roth 401(k) plans. There is a big difference

between tax deferral and tax avoidance. There will come a time when you will be very happy you have built up a significant amount of money in a *tax-free* account.

- **Find each fund's expense ratio in its prospectus.** It should be 0.50% or less, but that will occur only with index funds, EFTs, and passively managed funds. Avoid high-cost funds.

- **Avoid any annuity offered through your 401(k).** They carry high costs and are generally a bad deal for plan participants.

This can be an eye-opening exercise. If your plan includes a selection of high-cost funds that don't use these benchmarks, and no index funds, invest the minimum necessary to obtain the maximum employer match. The contribution limits for individual IRAs and Roth IRAs are not affected by the amount you contribute to your 401(k) plan.

If there's no employer match, consider investing in a traditional IRA, a Roth IRA (if you qualify), or an after-tax account. With these investments, you control your investment options and can invest in a globally diversified portfolio of low management fee index funds (or ETFs) in an asset allocation appropriate for your tolerance for risk.

Many employers don't understand how bad their plans are for employees. If you ask your plan administrator in human resources (or the president, in a small company) to request a fee audit, they might see what's going on and make some changes. In a large company, you might join the committee that makes plan decisions. Or you might point out (gently) that some companies have faced class action suits over their plans.

The ABCs of IRAs

Congress created IRAs to encourage retirement savings. Traditional IRAs (as opposed to Roth IRAs) encourage savings by allowing you to contribute up to $5,000 a year *pre-tax* to the account (or up to $6,000 if you're at least 50 years old).

The amount you contribute in a year is 100% deductible from that year's taxes. In fact, you can make contributions and deduct them from your previous tax year's income through April 15. Taxes on your contributions and returns are deferred until you make withdrawals.

But there is a downside:

- You must start taking minimum annual distributions when you reach age 70½ or face steep penalties.

- You may face a penalty of 10% of the amount withdrawn if you withdraw cash before age 59½. Check for exceptions, which include the use of IRA money to pay higher-education expenses or to help purchase your first home.

- You must pay taxes at your marginal income tax rate on the entire amount you withdraw on the date you withdraw it.

For those reasons, provided you qualify (as explained below), consider a Roth IRA. The contribution limits are the same as those governing traditional IRAs, but a Roth has the following benefits:

- You don't have to take distributions when you reach age 70½, if the plan has been in existence for at least five years.

- You don't have to pay any taxes on withdrawals from your Roth account once you reach age 59 ½, if the plan has been in existence for at least five years.

Not everyone qualifies for a full contribution to a Roth. In 2011, if you're a single head of household or married filing separately, your income cannot exceed $122,000. If you're married and filing jointly, it cannot exceed $179,000. (Here *income* means modified adjusted gross income from IRS Form 1040. See IRS Publication 590, Individual Retirement Arrangements, for the most recent rules.)

Whichever IRA you choose, it can be an alternative or a supplement to a 401(k) plan. You'll have better investment options and better returns and, provided you arrange for monthly automatic transfers into the IRA or Roth, you will save just as regularly.

🌿 mint hint

John Jagerson's post "The Hidden Costs of Your 401(k)" (www.mint .com/blog/investing/the-hidden -costs-of-your-401k) contains additional information on these broker-enrichment schemes. In addition, Mint.com's "Ways to Save" section can assist you in identifying and setting up attractive IRAs, as well as rolling over your 401(k) plan into an IRA—when appropriate— to reduce the high expenses associated with these accounts.

Don't Be Fooled

Having your employer set you up in a 401(k) plan or deferring taxes in a traditional IRA may seem attractive. But if your employer doesn't match your 401(k) contribution, and has the typical fare of high expense ratio, actively managed funds as investment options, avoid it. If you don't need the tax breaks of a traditional IRA, go for a Roth if you're eligible. If you participate in your 401(k) plan, and it has a Roth option, seriously consider it.

Also, if you can save beyond the IRA and Roth limits, after-tax accounts invested in low management fee index funds can be as good or better than a 401(k) plan or a traditional IRA.

What's the Point?

The high expenses and conflicts of interest in employer-sponsored 401(k) and similar plans can cost you a good part of your returns, so carefully consider the pros and cons and your alternatives.

CHAPTER 35

Making Your Money Outlive You

Despite increasing signs of a stabilizing U.S. economy, 19 percent
of Americans—including 17 percent of full-time workers—have
been compelled to take money from their retirement savings in
the last year.
—Sheyna Steiner, financial journalist

Budgeting in the present—and for retirement—is a corner-
stone of retirement planning. If you find yourself dipping
into your retirement funds to meet expenses before you
retire, you clearly need to adjust your current spending or increase
your income. Once you actually retire, you'll have to exercise even
more control over your withdrawals.

I'm assuming you'll want to retire someday. The *Business
Insider* blog reports that "according to a recent AARP survey of
baby boomers, 40% of them plan to work 'until they drop'" and
"approximately 3 out of 4 Americans start claiming Social Security benefits the moment they are eligible at age 62." Meanwhile,
36% of Americans don't contribute to retirement savings, which
shouldn't be your problem if you've read this far. But once you
have a portfolio the challenge becomes making it last the rest of

your life. The guidelines in this chapter are straightforward, but you'll need to modify them for your situation. Because of the complexity of this issue, you should consider seeking assistance from a qualified financial adviser or accountant. I discussed these issues in more detail in *The Smartest Retirement Book You'll Ever Read*, which you may find a useful resource.

How Long Is the Future?

At birth, average American life expectancy is 78 years: 75 years for men and 80 years for women. The following table shows life expectancy by gender at various ages.

Age	Life Expectancy—Male	Life Expectancy—Female
30	77	81
40	78	82
50	79	82
60	81	84
70	84	86
80	88	89
90	94	95

The longer you live, the longer you're likely to live longer than the average. (I'm reminded of Mickey Mantle saying, "If I knew I was going to live this long, I'd have taken better care of myself." That could be paraphrased as, "If I knew I was going to live this long, I'd have managed my money better.")

If you have seen enough of the working world to know that you might like to opt out someday or you are about to retire or have already retired, you must decide how to withdraw funds from your portfolio in the most advantageous manner.

From Accumulation to Withdrawal

If you have more money that you can ever spend, congratulations. However, most people who have accumulated a sizable nest egg face serious decisions about how much to withdraw.

The common idea of living off the interest is a bit naive. For example, legendary fund manager Peter Lynch believed that retirees could annually withdraw slightly less than their historical returns. But a study showed that withdrawals of 7% or 8% a year could reduce a portfolio to zero in 13 years.

Withdrawing money from your portfolio can dramatically affect its performance. This is especially the case in the first few years of retirement. As demonstrated by the skidding stock markets of 1987, the late 1990s, and the late 2000s, market down cycles can dramatically impact portfolios.

Determining Withdrawal Amounts and Timing

The key factor determining how much you can withdraw from your portfolio is its annual performance, especially early in your retirement. If you retire before or during a bear market, seemingly reasonable withdrawals could diminish your portfolio. If you retire before or during a bull market, higher withdrawals may seem warranted.

Yet despite market conditions, you must shift to living mainly on investment income once you retire. How do you go about doing it while guarding your future investment income? Here are some guidelines:

- **The 2% to 4% rule:** William Bernstein said, "Two percent is bulletproof, 3 percent is probably safe, 4 percent is pushing it, and, at 5 percent, you're eating Alpo in your old age." If you limit your annual withdrawals to 2% to 4%, you'll be fine in bull markets and in bear markets.

- **The 4%-plus rule:** You limit withdraws to no more than 4.15% in your first year of retirement. For each subsequent year, you take the amount of the previous year's withdrawal and increase it by the annual inflation rate. For example, if you withdrew $40,000 in the previous year and the inflation rate was 3%, you could increase the withdrawal for the current year by $1,200. This rule of thumb works only if you have 50% to 75% of your portfolio in stock funds. If you're more conservatively invested, stick with the 2% to 4% rule.

- **The floor-and-ceiling rule:** William Bengen developed a floor-and-ceiling strategy for safe withdrawals. You start with a withdrawal of 5% and then follow a couple of rules. In a bull market, you can take up to 25% more than the initial year's withdrawal. In a bear market, you cut back to 90% of the initial withdrawal. This assumes withdrawals are taken at the beginning of the year. Bengen concluded that retirees using this approach had a 91% chance of having their portfolios last for 30 years.

Obviously, with any approach, the larger your portfolio, the higher the dollar amount of your withdrawals. What may be less obvious is that a disciplined system in which you use a baseline withdrawal rate of 2% to 5% and adjust for market conditions is the key to making your money last.

Withdrawal Sequencing Strategies

Most people have their retirement funds in various accounts—401(k) plans, IRAs, annuities, taxable accounts, and pensions.

mint hint

You can use the Mint.com "Save for Retirement" goal (https://www.mint.com/saving-money/long-term-goals) to get a quick idea of how much you need to save each month for your retirement. Simply input your current age, income, and play with the risk versus return knob, and Mint will do the rest.

The sequence in which you withdraw funds from accounts can affect how long your money lasts, although sometimes your choices are limited. For example, you must start withdrawals from a traditional IRA at age 70½.

Here is the basic order in which you should tap your accounts:

1. *Post-tax accounts*, which are funded with money that has already been taxed. Only the gains will be taxed, at the usually lower capital gains rate.

2. *Deferred retirement accounts*, such as 401(k)s and traditional IRAs. Withdrawals will be taxed at the income tax rate that applies to you at the time.

3. *Roth IRAs*, which are funded with after-tax dollars. Withdrawals of principal are not taxed, neither are investment earnings once you reach age 59½, if the plan has been in existence for at least five years. These funds aren't subject to compulsory withdrawals, so this should probably be the last account you tap.

Use these rules of thumb for planning your withdrawal strategy, but modify them for your situation to maximize the life of your money.

What's the Point?

When you retire, you need a plan for withdrawals so your money will last you and your spouse for the rest of your lives.

CHAPTER 36

Sources of Cash in Retirement

When I was young I thought that money was the most important
thing in life; now that I am old, I know that it is.
—Oscar Wilde, Irish author and playwright

I n or near retirement, you may face a severe financial setback or
simply find yourself without enough money to live as you
expected. If so, you have options. Some are more attractive
than others, and you'll make a better decision by carefully considering them rather than jumping on the first one that presents
itself.

First, be sure to assess the reason you need cash. Health issues
and basic necessities are clearly needs. But you don't need to help
a child buy a home or start a business. Nor do you need to take a
foreign vacation, remodel the basement, or keep up with the
Joneses.

When you *need* money in excess of your withdrawals, how
you obtain it can make the difference between financial security
and being wiped out. This chapter examines ways of raising
cash from the equity in your home and a few other options.

Avoid Reverse Mortgages

Reverse mortgage loans have become increasingly popular, with over 660,000 made from 1990 to 2010. However, like any huge pool of assets, home equity has become a magnet for vultures in the financial services industry. I recommend avoiding a reverse mortgage loan, except as a last resort. (Recently major players in the reverse mortgage game, such as Bank of America and Wells Fargo, have withdrawn from this endeavor, citing "unpredictable home values.")

A reverse mortgage enables anyone who is at least 62 to tap their home equity for 50% to 70% of the home's value, provided the mortgage is paid off or nearly paid off. You can sometimes use the proceeds of the reverse mortgage loan to pay off a low balance.

To obtain a reverse mortgage, you must live in the home and meet certain Housing and Urban Development (HUD) criteria. The amount you'll receive depends on several factors, including your age, the interest rate, and your home's appraised value. You don't have to make repayments and you can use the money for any purpose. You retain title to your home and the lender is repaid when you sell it or your estate sells it.

This may sound like a good deal, but it usually isn't. The fees are exorbitant—about 8% to 10% of your home's value (not the loan value)—and include an origination fee, mortgage insurance premiums, and the usual slew of closing costs. Since the loan is a percentage of your home's value, you'd almost certainly obtain more cash and better your financial situation if you sold it and moved to less expensive quarters.

See HUD's information on these mortgages (www.hud./gov/buying/rvrsmort.cfm) and go to AARP's site (www.aarp.org) for additional information.

Better Ways to Tap Home Equity

Here are four potentially better ways to tap your home equity:

- **Refinance your home:** If you have a mortgage and interest rates are favorable, consider refinancing. It will cost less and preserve more of your home's value as an asset to you and your spouse and heirs.

- **Home equity loan:** A home equity loan or line of credit usually features low fees. Home equity loans and refinancing can usually be done easier, faster, and cheaper than a reverse mortgage or sale of your home. But you'll face monthly loan payments.

- **Home Equity Conversion Mortgage (HECM) Saver Loan:** This HUD program, started in 2010 and run by a private lender, *can* be a good alternative to a standard reverse mortgage. Up-front fees are usually low but the loan amount is also usually lower and interest can be higher.

- **Sell your home:** Consider selling your home if it is too big for your present needs or you face high repair costs (or are forgoing repairs) or high taxes (even with a senior discount). If you sell, you can downsize and then rent an apartment or buy a reasonable condo.

Selling your home to your child may be an option, but can lead you to sell for less than market value. In general, carefully consider any "family solution" to a financial problem. Family issues can make such problems difficult to see clearly. If you have financial problems, seek financial solutions while remaining open to help from loved ones.

Other Options and Issues

If you are facing financial stress before or during retirement (or at other times), you have options other than tapping your home equity:

- **Cash value life insurance:** You can often obtain a loan against a whole or universal life policy. If you don't repay it, the amount will be deducted from your death benefit. You may also be able to take a lump sum in lieu of the death benefit. There are many costs and risks associated with borrowing against your cash value insurance. Before making this decision, it would be best to speak with a fee-only insurance adviser.

- **Consider using an IRA rollover to "borrow" money:** While IRA loans are not permitted, you have wiggle room if you use a 60-day rollover, but be very careful. You can withdraw money from your IRA or Roth without taxes or penalties *if* you redeposit the funds within 60 days. If you miss this deadline, you must pay the taxes and penalties. You can do this once a year from the same IRA. If you are in distress, this solution applies *only* if you are certain you can repay within 60 days.

- **Borrow from your 401(k) rather than take an early IRA withdrawal:** If your company permits you to borrow from your 401(k), you can typically borrow up to 50% of the vested assets in your account, up to $50,000. Check your plan for all rules. Generally, you must repay the loan through payroll deductions, and if you lose your job, you must pay the loan within 60 days or face a tax bill.

Rather than face an under-funded retirement, it may be better to delay retirement and step up your savings, or delay taking Social Security. Although you can file for your Social Security benefits at age 62—and three out of four people now do—research has shown that for each year you delay filing, your payments will increase 7% to 8%.

mint hint

See "Reverse Mortgages Explained" by Michael C. Thomsett for more information on these mortgages and their costs (www .mint.com/blog/how-to/reverse -mortgage-02222011).

What's the Point?

You have sources of cash if you are near or in retirement, but you need to evaluate your options carefully.

PART TEN

Life (and Death) Events

Major challenges such as child rearing, illness, and death have financial implications that you can gauge and plan for ahead of time. Anticipating these events in your financial plan will make it stronger and more flexible. If some of your money does outlive you, you may want a portion of it to go to your favorite charities.

This part anticipates the financial effects of major life events and will help you consider the legacy you will leave in your estate plan.

CHAPTER 37

Kids Cost Money

I know I can provide my son with a high-quality life and maintain ours. But I think a second child would break us.
—Vanessa Martin, mother of one

I n the Southern California Valley Girl slang of the 1980s, teenagers from well-off homes would refer to Dad as "The Wallet" or to either parent as "The ATM." Their glib portrayal of parents as fountains of cash pointed to a deeper truth—kids cost money.

A study by the U.S. Department of Agriculture found that the total cost of raising one child from birth through age 17 is $222,000 for a family with an average income of $76,000. For families with incomes above $98,000 that figure rises to $369,000. Neither of these figures includes college.

Few things raise your monetary metabolic burn rate higher than children. Increased housing costs are the biggest hit, with child care and education next. Married parents spend an average of 40% more on entertainment, 16% more on groceries, and 40% more on clothing and shoes.

Few things bring more joy in life than children. Very few parents would, in retrospect, choose not to become parents, regardless of the cost. But how do you have children without impoverishing yourself?

Think Financially

The decision to have a child, and each subsequent child, is an emotional decision with financial impact. People downplay the financial aspects until hard times hit. "Years ago, people didn't really think about how many children they were having—they just kind of had them," says Susan Newman, author of *Parenting an Only Child*. "There are still people who say money isn't the issue, but they are fewer and farther between now."

Given the massive costs, you should know what you're getting into and plan accordingly:

- **Housing:** Seeking more space and better schools, many city dwellers move to the suburbs after having a child. The town you live in largely determines your housing costs. Check out *Bloomberg Businessweek*'s annual survey "Best Places to Raise a Family" for more information.

- **Daycare and lost income:** To spend time with an infant or toddler, one parent in a two-income couple will often leave his or her job or cut back. Calculate the income you will forgo and prepare to get by on less. If you'll use daycare or after-school care, shop the costs, which vary widely by state. Full-time daycare for a four-year-old child ranges from $3,750 in Mississippi to $11,450 in Massachusetts. Nearby family can help, but that's not always a fair or practical solution.

- **K–12 education:** Although the correlation between outlay per student and measures like standardized test scores and college admission is high, school systems provide varying value for tax dollars. Compare school districts using town websites and resources like NeighborhoodScout.com, a short-term subscription service. Private schools may offer better-quality education but usually at far greater cost than the higher property taxes in good public school districts. However, high property taxes don't ensure good schools. Parental involvement is also key.

- **College:** Some parents feel they owe their child a college education, while others believe students should pay their way and will work harder when they do. A mix of parent and child funding and loans tends to work for many families. Motivated students can often get as good an education at a good state school as at a private one. Community colleges and military service also offer low-cost paths to four-year degrees.

Saving for College?

Thinking of taking on debt for your child's education? CPA Sally Herigstad recommends that you don't, pointing out that "your kids can get student loans, but there's no such thing as a retirement loan."

College tuition accounts, such as 529 plans, can be bad deals. Named for an Internal Revenue Code section, 529 plans allow you to save for college with tax-deferred growth on deposits, protection from bankruptcy, and the ability to use the funds at almost any U.S. college and many abroad.

But this federal plan is administered by the states and plan sponsors. The investment strategies, tax benefits, and incentives vary wildly. Many plans feature an ugly lineup of fees—"fund expenses, state fees, program manager fees, miscellaneous fees, annual distribution fees, total annual asset based fees, and account maintenance costs are all associated with 529 accounts," according to Scholarships.com. If your child doesn't go to college and you put the money to other purposes, you lose all the tax benefits.

You can undermine your children's chances of getting financial aid by saving for their tuition, particularly if you put the funds in their name. Keep the money in your name so they can apply for financial aid without factoring in any resources you may provide.

mint hint

"Education Savings 101: Ways to Save" by Donna Fuscaldo provides an excellent overview of college savings plans, including Coverdell Education Savings Accounts (ESAs) and Uniform Gifts to Minors and Uniform Transfers to Minors (www .mint.com/blog/goals/education -savings-101-ways-to-save). There is also a Mint.com goal called "Save for College," which asks just three questions: child's age; public in-state, public out-of-state, or private school; and money saved so far to come up with a monthly savings target for your child's educational expenses. When you're setting up an educational goal, Mint will recommend savings options—like 529 plans—best suited for your goal.

More Responsibility

Finally, there is the responsibility of raising kids who can handle financial matters. This goes beyond helping them set up a lemonade stand and open a bank account (good things, to be sure!). It means discussing money openly, teaching them calmly about financial decisions, and letting them see you make good ones.

Take the mystery out of money by showing them how to draw up a budget, track their spending, save for future purchases, and invest wisely. Show them how to allocate money to what they really value, and how to put their money to work for them.

Teaching your child how to make, spend, save, and invest money is more valuable than any money you could give them. Be particularly careful if you have substantial wealth. If you do, check out the information and programs at Independent Means Inc.

What's the Point?

Consider all the financial effects of having each child and plan to manage the impact.

CHAPTER 38

Giving Back

*I resolved to stop accumulating and begin the infinitely more
serious and difficult task of wise distribution.*
—Andrew Carnegie, American industrialist

Charitable giving should ideally include donations of time, talent, and treasure, as charities put it. But the tax code deals only with the treasure part—to good effect. According to the National Philanthropic Trust, in 2009 about 65% of households gave to charity, while 27% of the population volunteered.

This chapter covers charitable giving, or philanthropy. For IRS purposes, a charitable organization or qualifying charity is defined by section 501(c)(3) of the tax code. Not all nonprofits fit the definition.

Always consider the tax effects of your donations. When you donate to charity, gains on assets are often not recognized as income or gains to you. Yet often you can *within limits* obtain income tax deductions for an asset's fair market value. Timing of gifts can have tax consequences as well.

Charitable giving can help you avoid leaving enough to your heirs to spoil them, if that is a concern. Certain types of trusts can also deal with this issue, as discussed in Chapter 40. If the notion of having large sums to donate to charity seems remote, think first in small sums so you develop the habit of giving back as part of managing your finances. Also, if you follow the advice in this book from an early age, you will almost certainly have money to donate to charity in your later years.

Ways to Give

Here are four ways to leave money to charitable organizations:

Lump-Sum Gift

An outright gift is simpler than planned giving, but not always practical in your lifetime if you depend on income from the assets. An outright gift removes the assets from your estate, which can lower estate taxes. You can donate in a single year or stagger a gift over several years. Speak with your tax adviser about the most beneficial strategy, while considering the charity's needs. (Most charities are small, and only 0.4% have assets over $100 million.)

Charitable Gift Annuity

A charitable gift annuity resembles an immediate annuity (Chapter 19). You buy an annuity and donate it to the charity, which collects the principal when you die. During your lifetime, you receive fixed payments. These payments will be less than those of an immediate annuity, but more than you'd get from a certificate of deposit. The older you are, the higher your fixed payments will be.

Charitable gift annuities have meaningful tax benefits. You get a charitable contribution deduction for the gift portion of the amount transferred. The amount of the deduction requires a somewhat complicated calculation of the "present value of the remainder interest" of the annuity and is best left to your tax adviser.

A portion of the payments you receive are taxable as ordinary income and the remaining portion is deemed to be a tax-free return of your principal.

These annuities can also be attractive if you own stock that has appreciated but is not generating dividends. If you sold the stock, you'd be taxed at the capital gains rate. The annuity lets you give the stock to the charity and collect payments over time, portions of which may be tax free, or taxed at ordinary income or capital gains rates.

There are other tax ramifications of charitable gift annuities, so be sure to discuss all aspects of this gift with the charity and your tax adviser. Annuity rates are "suggested" by the American Council on Gift Annuities (www.acga-web.org) and change annually. IRS rules are also subject to change.

Donor Advised Fund

Donor advised funds enable various unrelated donors to have the same core organization administer and invest funds for charitable giving. In 2009, there were more than 152,000 holders of donor advised funds, which held some $25 billion in assets. Annual contributions to these funds totaled $5.9 billion that year.

You can contribute as little as $10,000 to a donor advised fund, but control over the investments and the grants to charities ultimately belongs to the fund. You obtain an income tax deduction for up to 50% of your adjusted gross income on cash contributions and up to 30% on long-term appreciation of assets (including real estate). Valuing your contribution for tax purposes can be complex, so consult your tax adviser regarding contributions to a donor advised fund.

The tax advantages can be significant. Here's an example contrasting two distinct options: selling appreciated securities and donating the cash to a charity, and donating appreciated securities rather than cash to a charity (from Vanguard's website). Suppose you paid $10,000 for securities now worth $100,000.

Sell Securities and Donate Cash	Donate Securities
Pay 15% capital gains tax on the $90,000 appreciation ($13,500)	Pay no capital gains tax
Deduct $100,000 from taxable income	Deduct $100,000 from taxable income
Save $35,000 in income tax (at tax rate of 35%)	Save $35,000 in income tax (at tax rate of 35%)
Charity receives $100,000	Charity receives $100,000
After-tax cost to you: $78,500	After-tax cost to you: $65,000

Here are the web pages for three major fund families' donor advised funds:

Vanguard
www.vanguardcharitable.org

Fidelity Funds
http://charitablegift.org

T. Rowe Price
www.programforgiving.org/charitable/pages/home.jsp

Research and compare all fees, costs, and returns and speak with your financial adviser before donating. You'll find a tool to help calculate charitable deductions at PhilanthroCalc for the Web (http://pcalc.ptec.com).

Charitable Remainder Trust

A charitable remainder trust is an irrevocable trust that distributes a fixed percentage of its assets to you or to a beneficiary,

mint hint

See "Charity: Who Cares?" for interesting, well-presented statistics on U.S. charitable giving (www .mint.com/blog/trends/charity -who-cares).

such as a spouse, as an annuity while you are alive. When you die, the trust pays the remaining balance to the designated charity (hence the term *remainder*).

The fixed payments must total 5% to 50% of the value of the trust's assets. The amount that goes to charity must be at least 10% of the assets contributed to the trust. You avoid capital gains tax on the donated assets and get them out of your estate.

There are various forms of these trusts, with different tax effects, which you should discuss with your financial adviser and estate planning attorney. Chapter 40 covers basic types of trusts.

Check Out Your Charities

Before you donate, visit Charity Navigator (www.charitynaviga tor.org). This independent site evaluates more than 5,500 of America's largest charities and answers questions about salaries, administrative costs, and other areas of interest to donors.

What's the Point?

Charitable giving has many advantages, not the least of which is making a meaningful contribution to those in need.

CHAPTER 39

In Sickness and in Wealth

La vecchiaia è strega. (Old age is a witch.)
—Italian proverb

Most aging people have said, "I never want to end up in a nursing home." Yet nursing homes are full—and they're not cheap. The average annual cost of a private nursing home room was $85,775 in 2011. Having a roommate knocked that down to about $75,000.

Cost isn't the only issue. People are also concerned about quality of care (and food), and about living in an institutional setting. Staying at home is an option for elderly people with family they can depend on or who can afford home health aides and visiting nurses. While it's a fraction of the cost of a nursing home, care at home also costs money:

- Home health aides cost $21 to $30 an hour.

- Daily stays in an adult daycare center cost an average of $67.

- Average monthly rates in an assisted living community are about $3,300.

At least 70% of people over 65 will require long-term care services at some point. Contrary to what most people believe, private health insurance (covered in Chapter 20) and Medicare *do not* pay for most long-term care services, although Medicare does pay for some as I explain below. That means if you need long-term nursing home care you must pay your own way, unless you have long-term care insurance.

What Medicare Covers

Medicare program details are subject to change, but the program currently pays for care in a skilled nursing facility *if* you had a recent hospital stay of at least three days, and *if* you're admitted to a Medicare-certified nursing facility within 30 days, and *if* you need nursing care or physical or other therapy on your doctor's orders.

Under those circumstances Medicare covers 100% of the first 20 days, and then you pay up to $141.50 (in 2011) a day of your expenses for days 21 to 100. After 100 days, you or your long-term care insurer, or both, pay all expenses.

For home healthcare, Medicare pays for medically necessary part-time nursing care and home health aide services and for therapies and medical devices ordered by your doctor and provided by a Medicare-certified home health agency. There is no co-pay (except 20% for medical devices), and services continue as long as your doctor reorders them at least every 60 days. Hospice care is also covered by Medicare.

You may have heard stories of elderly people going through "asset-spend-down" to qualify for Medicaid, the state health insurance program for the needy. Some elderly people do enter nursing homes and pay their own way until they qualify for Medicaid. But proper planning can help you avoid that outcome.

Long-Term Care Insurance

Long-term care insurance is actively marketed to baby boomers and seniors, and you must be careful what you're buying. Insurance adviser Scott Witt notes: "My concern with long-term care is that the premiums for a policy that provides significant peace of mind are so expensive that most people end up buying a policy that provides little real protection against a catastrophic long-term care event."

In deciding whether to purchase long-term care insurance, you might consider your need based on these general net worth guidelines:

- **Below $200,000:** You'll probably rely on Medicaid for long-term care, although insurance would broaden your choice of facilities.

- **$200,000 to $750,000:** You'd have to deplete your assets before qualifying for Medicaid. Seriously consider a short-fat policy (explained below).

- **$750,000 to $2 million:** Though your stay wouldn't deplete your nest egg, you should still consider a short-fat policy (explained below).

- **Above $2 million:** You can pay your own way or consider a policy with a long elimination period with lifetime coverage or lifetime coverage with a high daily benefit (to obtain a higher level of care).

Choosing the Right Coverage

Your basic options are a short-fat policy, with a short period of coverage but higher daily benefits (e.g., $200 a day for three years), or a long-thin policy, with a longer period of coverage but lower daily benefits (e.g., $100 a day for six years).

Generally, short-fat is the way to go because the average nursing home stay is less than three years. You can claim less than your daily benefit under a short-fat policy and stretch out the coverage period. But you can't claim more than your daily benefit under the long-thin policy.

Key coverage considerations include:

- **Daily benefit:** You select the daily benefit, with an eye on local costs instead of national averages. See the National Clearinghouse for Long-Term Care Information (www.longtermcare.gov).

- **Elimination period:** This is the waiting period before your benefits kick in, such as 30, 60, 90, or 180 days, or even a year. Or you can buy a policy with no elimination period.

- **Inflation protection:** Although this is the most important option to include in a long-term care policy, it is often excluded because of its cost. With this option, your benefit increases to keep pace with inflation and increased cost of expenses.

- **Tax considerations:** Be sure your policy is federally qualified so that your benefits will be tax free.

As with any insurance policy, be certain you understand (not *think* you understand) the policy provisions *and* the costs. Many experts believe long-term care premiums may increase substantially on existing policies. This possibility should be factored into your decision-making process.

Be Sure You Can Afford It

Long-term care insurance isn't cheap, and the older you get, the higher the premiums become. Premiums are supposed to stay level, but a company can raise premiums for everyone in a class, such as a specific age group or residents of a specific state.

In 2010, the average buyer of long-term care insurance was 57 years old and the average annual premium for all ages was $2,150, according to the American Association for Long-Term Care Insurance. But according to the *Wall Street Journal* article reporting that figure, premiums have been soaring and in some cases approaching $5,000 a year.

Be sure to pick a policy you can afford because if you stop paying, your coverage lapses. A "non-forfeiture binder" will keep the benefit in effect for a shorter period if you stop paying premiums—but it can double your premium. Offered as an option, the non-forfeiture binder provides for payment of benefits if you cancel the policy. For example, if you paid $12,000 in premiums over four years and then canceled the policy, you would still be entitled to a daily benefit up to the amount of the premiums paid. So, if your policy had a daily benefit of $100, you'd be entitled to 120 days of benefits *if* you had paid extra for the non-forfeiture binder.

As with most insurance, you're betting on the likelihood of something bad happening or not happening, and on what it might cost you or your loved ones. Take your health, finances, and family situation into account when you bet—or choose not to bet—on long-term care insurance.

Deal with an insurer with an A rating or better, an excellent reputation, and a clean record with your state insurance regulator. Check the National Association of Insurance Commis-

mint hint

See the article "Health Care Reformed: What Will Change for You?" by Aleksandra Todorova for views on the healthcare legislation (www.mint.com/blog/trends/health-care-reform) and the related video "Good Health Care News for Some 20-Somethings" (found on the same page).

sioners at www.naic.org and click on "States Jurisdictions." Otherwise, getting claims paid could be difficult.

Medigap Insurance

Take the time you'll need to understand Medicare and weigh your options. Consider buying Medigap insurance. This is supplemental coverage for co-pays, deductibles, and other expenses not covered by Medicare. Medigap coverage is available to people who have Medicare Parts A and B but not to those who are on Part C (Medicare Advantage).

This area is complex and rapidly changing, but Medicare and Medigap insurance resources at AARP (www.aarp.org) offer timely, reliable information.

What's the Point?

Long-term care insurance can provide peace of mind, but be sure you purchase the policy that's right for you.

CHAPTER 40

Estate Planning Basics

**Family wealth is not self-perpetuating. Without careful planning
and stewardship, a hard-earned fortune can easily be dissipated
within a generation or two.**
—James E. Hughes Jr., attorney and author

You can't take it with you—and the way you leave it behind
in your estate plan can make life better or worse for your
heirs. Few people enjoy thinking about estate planning.
However, you have a responsibility to your heirs and to future
generations. Careful planning will help you meet them.

The estate planning you'll require depends on the amount
and type of assets you have and how you intend to distribute
them. If you have significant assets—particularly an operating
business or income-generating real estate—your estate plan will
be more complex than one that simply conveys a home and a
portfolio to your heirs and beneficiaries. However, even a simple
plan demands thought.

An estate plan consists of legal documents, a will, and, often, a
trust, which instructs the executor of your estate how you want
your assets distributed, how you're addressing situations such as
ongoing care for a disabled child, and how other final wishes
such as funeral arrangements should be carried out.

This chapter discusses basic estate planning considerations and mistakes to avoid. Be wary of using forms off the web and other do-it-yourself estate planning devices. You need an experienced estate planning attorney to develop a good plan.

Wills, Trusts, and Probate

Many people put off making a will and die intestate, which means without a will. If you have a will, it will go through probate. That court-overseen process ensures that the will is valid, its provisions are carried out, and claims against the estate (such as creditors' claims) are settled.

If there's no will, the probate court distributes the assets and settles claims. You don't want that to happen. States charge fees for the process, which is impersonal and open to the public. A will also becomes public through probate, but a trust is not a public document and can provide greater privacy. A trust, which owns assets before or after your death (or both), can also provide greater flexibility and control.

Estate Planning Mistakes

Most people have their family lawyer draw up a fairly standard document. That can cause mistakes, which I've flagged in the table below, along with suggestions on how to avoid them.

Estate Planning Mistake	How to Avoid It
Basing the plan only on tax considerations	Consider family members' specific needs and how they will handle assets
Choosing the wrong executor or trustee	Appoint an executor or trustee with compassion, maturity, and experience; consider a professional trustee

Estate Planning Mistake	How to Avoid It
Leaving heirs unprepared to handle assets	Prepare heirs for their responsibilities, and don't leave assets to irresponsible ones
Putting a sibling in charge of other siblings' finances	Have the trustee ensure that children are treated according to the trust's provisions
Leaving successors unprepared to own and manage a business	Plan succession or sell the business if heirs can't or don't want to own and manage it
Failing to update documents as circumstances change	Update documents and beneficiaries for marriages, divorces, births, etc.

Many estate planners focus mainly on avoiding the estate tax, which has historically increased and decreased. The amount of the deceased's assets exempt from the tax rose to $1.5 million in 2005, $2 million in 2006 to 2008, and $3.5 million in 2009. The tax rate fell from 47% to 46% to 45% in those periods. In 2010, the estate tax fell to zero. For 2011 and 2012, the exemption was raised to $5 million and the rate dropped to 35%.

It is likely that the estate tax will keep changing. Although estate tax rates are high, mismanagement of assets by unknowledgeable or irresponsible family members often does more damage to wealth than taxes. You can't control your heirs from the grave (or urn), but you can leave an estate plan that reflects your best efforts to truly help them while preserving assets when you are gone.

Basic Estate Planning Tools

You distribute your assets with a will and a trust, and by naming beneficiaries to your various retirement and bank accounts.

- A *will* sets forth the manner in which you want your assets distributed after your death. Legally, a will is all you usually need to convey assets to heirs and beneficiaries, but various trusts have been created to serve a range of purposes.

- A *trust* holds your assets for another party, usually with instructions and, depending on the trust, certain features. For example, a generation-skipping trust (GST) can let your child receive the returns on a portfolio but leave the portfolio to your grandchild(ren). (A living, or revocable, trust is one you create while you're alive and can change rather than one created at your death or that is irrevocable.) You convey ownership of the assets to the trust, but you control the trust (unless it is irrevocable). After you die, the trustee you appoint oversees the disposition of assets under the provisions of the trust.

- *Naming beneficiaries* to your retirement and bank accounts is straightforward. When you open a 401(k) or IRA, you name the beneficiary, and they receive the assets in it when you die. Ask your financial adviser, mutual fund firm, and bank for the forms needed to name beneficiaries and to establish a payable-on-death account or transfer-on-death registration.

Types of irrevocable trusts include exemption trusts (for taking advantage of the estate tax exemption), life insurance trusts (for holding life insurance policies and their proceeds), qualified terminable interest property (QTIP) trusts (for transferring assets to a spouse using the marital deduction), and the above-mentioned GST. I won't explain these here and instead have listed resources that do in Part Twelve.

Final Thoughts

When preparing a will or trust, consider *all* your assets, including real estate, businesses, art, coin collections and other valuables, and memorabilia. The more clearly you make your wishes known, the better. If you believe provisions of your estate plan will cause resentment or controversy among your heirs, it's typically best to explain what you're doing and why before you die. It can defuse the emotions that lead to contested wills.

As always, where there's a pool of assets you'll find vultures from the financial services industry. In this case they include:

- Estate planning attorneys who will steer you to the banks, trust companies, and life insurance companies with whom they have mutual referral relationships.

- Trust companies and investment funds who will claim that they can generate market-beating returns, if you place your assets in trust with them.

- Insurance salespeople who, like the man with a hammer who sees mostly nails, will tell you that life insurance is the solution to most estate planning problems, when in fact it is only one option.

Trust companies make most of their money from advisory fees on your assets, not on trust administration fees. This not only subjects your assets to high fees but also creates a conflict of interest because the same company tries to act as both trustee and investment manager. How closely is the trustee going to review itself as investment manager? This arrangement is the perfect storm for your estate: conflicts of interest and active management of your assets.

Here's how to avoid this problem. It's not advice you are likely to receive from your estate planning lawyer or other advisers.

Insist that your trust be managed by a directed trustee—a trust administrator who administers only trusts and does not manage money. There aren't many directed trustees, so you will need to do some research to find one. Some of the leading firms are Advisory Trust of Delaware, which is owned by Wilmington Trust (http://advisorytrustco.com), Santa Fe Trust (http://santafe trust.com), and the Charles Schwab Bank (http://content.schwab .com/sac/ats/home.html).

Once you have appointed a directed trustee, you will need to include language in your trust documents that directs the administrator to appoint a financial adviser who will use low management fee index funds and make no effort to beat the market through active management. This is essential to family wealth preservation. Here's language I recommend you insert into your trust document. Unless you insist on it, it's unlikely your advisers will suggest it. Failure to insert it means that your assets will most likely be actively managed, which defeats the purpose of appointing a directed trustee:

> mint hint
>
> Mint.com offers links to useful ebooks (www.mint.com/blog/finance-core/30-free-ebooks-to-learn-everything-you-want-to-know-about-personal-finance), including the Federal Trade Commission's pamphlet "Living Trust Offers: How to Make Sure They're Trustworthy."

The Investment Manager shall be guided by the basic principle known as Modern Portfolio Theory. The Investment Manager should make no effort to "beat the markets."

The Investment Manager shall focus on the asset allocation of the portfolio. The portfolio shall be globally diversified, using low management fee stock and bond index funds, exchange traded funds, or passively managed funds. The Investment Manager shall be guided by the principles set forth in *The Intelligent Asset Allocator* by William Bernstein, *A Random Walk Down Wall Street* by

Burton Malkiel, *The Little Book of Common Sense Investing* by John Bogle, and *The Smartest Investment Book You'll Ever Read* and *The Smartest Portfolio You'll Ever Own*, both by Daniel R. Solin.

Shouldn't your money work just as hard for your heirs as it did for you?

What's the Point?

Preparing your estate plan is one of the most financially smart and caring things you can do for your loved ones.

PART ELEVEN

Putting It All Together

A wealth-building plan improves control over your finances and your financial future. There are several moving parts to the plan, and you must get them to work together to achieve your goals. This part provides steps and tips that will help you to do that.

I close this part with eleven rules for personal financial management. Follow them and you will—despite the tireless efforts of those who want to separate you from your money—build wealth.

CHAPTER 41

Get a Budget

First we make our habits and then our habits make us.
—Charles C. Noble, British church organist (1812–1885)

Step 1. Set Your Goals

Set short-term and long-term goals, and for each one:

- Name your goal.

- Assign a dollar value to it.

- Set a target date for reaching it.

- Allocate monthly savings toward that goal.

- Set milestones—amounts and dates—to measure your progress.

Step 2. Assess Your Situation

Gather your financial information from your checkbook, investment accounts, receipts, and other sources, and:

- List your spending categories and amounts and compare with ideal budgets.

- Analyze your spending patterns: What are you spending your money on?

- Decide which course to take: How would you like to change your spending and saving?

Step 3. Write and Launch Your Plan

Once you have set your goals and made decisions about reaching them, you can decide *how* to go about it.

- Decide whether you can start saving now or will first pay down your debt.

- Prioritize cutbacks: Where can you cut back, by how much, and by when?

- Define your other priorities:
  - Opening an automatic savings account.
  - Opening an investment account.
  - Purchasing health and life insurance.

- Contact a fee-only financial or insurance adviser, if you need one.

Step 4. Track Your Progress

Organized—or online—record keeping is essential:

- Decide whether to use a hard copy, software (e.g., Quicken), or online system (Mint.com) to track your spending and saving.

- Make the system easy for you to use.

- Schedule a specific time to review your spending and saving each month.

- Reward yourself for progress.

- If you falter, adjust your plan or your spending behavior— don't give up.

Tips for Budgeting

- **Consider Mint.com.** Especially if you find the expense tracking and record keeping tedious or overwhelming.

- **Look at budgeting as decision making.** Budgeting is choosing what you want *more* and deciding when you can get it.

- **Get your loved ones on board.** If you have a family or partner, involve him or her in this process. You can't do it alone if you have other people in your life.

- **Get help if you need it.** The *right* financial planner, investment adviser, or life coach can help you with budgeting and priorities if you need help.

What's the Point?

Think of a budget like a map. Without it, you won't get to your destination.

CHAPTER 42

Get Out of Debt

Debt: An ingenious substitute for the chain and whip of the
slave driver.
—Ambrose Bierce, American journalist

Step 1. Pull It Together

Gather your credit card statements, car payment booklets, checkbook, and other records in one place.

Step 2. Sort It Out

Classify your debt by type (credit card, student loan, etc.), payment size, interest rate, and costs (late fees, membership fees, etc.). Add up the monthly and annual cost of each loan in fees and other costs, and in principal, and list them in order.

Step 3. Get It Prioritized

Decide which of your loans and credit cards you are going to pay off first, then second, then third, etc. *Consider* moving your high-interest credit card balances to lower-interest cards, or a home equity debt-consolidation loan.

Step 4. Budget the Money

Dedicate the greatest amount you can afford in your budget to accelerated debt reduction.

Step 5. Pay It Off

Set a schedule over the next two, three, four, or even five years, check on your progress every month, quarter, and year. Tear up all but one credit card and pay off the new charges *every single month*.

Tips for Debt Reduction

- **Postpone saving, if you must.** You may have to use money you'd rather be saving to reduce your debt. That's okay. Every time you make an extra payment on an 18% credit card loan you are saving money.

- **Set a realistic time frame.** It may take a few years to get out of debt, since it took a few years to get into it. The time will pass and you will be free of debt.

- **Pay off the costliest debt first.** You may be tempted to pay off the lowest balance first to get it off your books. But the goal is to reduce the money you're spending on your debt, as well as your debt.

- **Get help if you need it.** *Legitimate* credit counselors and debt management plans have helped thousands of people to get out of debt. I've mentioned resources in the chapters in Part Three and in the notes to those chapters in Part Twelve.

What's the Point?

The elimination of debt is critical to building wealth and financial security.

CHAPTER 43

Get a Home

A good home must be made, not bought.
—Joyce Maynard, American author

Step 1. Do Your Research

Research places to live—at the state, metropolitan, and neighbor-hood levels—and consider houses, apartments, and condomin-iums.

Step 2. Assess Your Costs

Project all of the housing costs associated with your top choices.

Step 3. Consider Renting Versus Buying

Carefully consider the rent versus buy decision, factoring in the housing market, your personal preference, and your finances.

Step 4. Revisit Your Housing Budget

Revisit and realistically budget your housing expenses. If they are (or will be) more than 20% to 25% of your total expenses, decide whether it's worthwhile. If it is, you must reduce other expenses.

Step 5. Shop for Money

If you need a mortgage, shop carefully, negotiate fees and expenses, and push for the best deal you can. It's a competitive market and they want your business.

Step 6. Do Your Homework

If you are buying, investigate the history and condition of the property, and the finances of any condo association, before you buy.

Step 7. Pay It Off

Before and after you buy, figure out the fastest way you can comfortably have your house paid off.

Tips for Managing Housing Expenses

- **Be a bargain hunter.** Be on the lookout for up-and-coming or recently rehabilitated neighborhoods, but be sure the property is not overpriced.

- **Keep your head.** You won't decide where to live and what to live in based only on the numbers, but running them will help you decide what you can afford—even if you fall in love with a property.

- **Watch your monetary metabolism.** As a major purchase and investment, a home can boost your expenses as well as your net worth. Be sure you can handle the payments and costs, or you may become a distressed homeowner.

- **Get great advice.** Particularly if you're seeking a short-sale or foreclosed property, have a local Realtor and an attorney on *your* team. The seller's Realtor and attorney do not represent your interests.

What's the Point?

Doing the rent versus buy analysis is critical, but I have never known a homeowner, *with a paid-off mortgage*, who had second thoughts.

CHAPTER 44

Get Insured

For almost 70 years the life insurance industry has been a smug
sacred cow feeding the public a steady line of sacred bull.
—Ralph Nader, attorney and consumer activist

Step 1. Consider Disability Insurance

Disability insurance provides income if illness or an injury prevents
you from working. The loss of income is exacerbated by the fact that
you may have additional medical bills and other needs. You may be
eligible for workers' compensation benefits, state disability insurance programs (available in a few states only), and Social Security
disability. Your employer may sponsor group insurance coverage. If
so, you should check the limits of that coverage. Most employees
will need to purchase individual disability insurance. You can use a
disability insurance needs calculator to determine how much
income you will have to replace. You will find one at www.life
happens.org/disability-insurance-needs-calculator.

Step 2. Decide Whether You Need Life Insurance

If you have no dependents, do you want insurance so you'll be
insurable (under that policy) in the future? If that's not an issue,
maybe you can postpone the purchase.

Step 3. Calculate Your Life Insurance Coverage

Use a needs-based approach to calculate your death benefit. You can also use an income-replacement guide, such as 10, 20, or 25 times your annual pay, and compare the results.

Step 4. Choose Your Policy Type

When you've calculated your coverage, decide whether you want a term or cash value policy. If you want cash value, choose between whole life and universal life. Insurance company websites and Mint.com can be valuable resources.

Step 5. Get Quotes

Contact three or four highly rated insurance companies (A rated by A. M. Best) for the coverage and type of policy you want. Be sure to include at least two mutual, rather than stock, companies.

Step 6. Stick with It

When you're comfortable with the role of insurance in your plan, keep paying the premiums. If you're not comfortable, adjust your coverage or policy type. Be alert to any changes in the company or its reputation or rating.

Tips on Insurance

- **Don't ignore insurance—or overreact.** It's easy to overlook this part of your plan, and then to discover it and make mistakes. Most people are either underinsured or have purchased the wrong policies for their needs.

- **Consider a cash value policy.** The advice to "buy term and invest the difference" is useful only if you invest the difference. If you know you won't, get a whole life or universal life policy. I don't know anyone who bought the *right* cash value policy and built up significant cash value who regrets making this decision.

- **Be skeptical.** Triple-check everything an insurance agent tells you. While few are dishonest, most believe deeply in life insurance and tend to favor products with higher commissions.

- **Get an independent opinion.** Have a fee-only insurance adviser examine the structure of any significant cash value policy or annuity you buy. Many points are negotiable, but it takes an expert to know which ones are.

What's the Point?

Insurance is a major purchase and a trap for the unwary and ill-informed. A fee-only insurance adviser levels the playing field.

CHAPTER 45

Get Invested

None of us is as smart as all of us.
—A sign at Wells Fargo Bank during the creation of the index fund,
circa 1971

Step 1. Define Your Goal

Calculate how large a portfolio you will need to retire on based on your projected income needs and other sources of income, such as a 401(k), pension, annuity, and Social Security. Target a realistic retirement date.

Step 2. Decide on Your Asset Allocation

The portion of your assets you allocate to stock and bond index funds depends on your time horizon and liquidity needs, income and savings rate, net worth, attitude toward risk, and knowledge of investing. The maximum standard deviation for the total portfolio of a conservative, moderately aggressive, or aggressive investor should be 8%, 15%, or 20%, respectively.

Step 3. Open an Account with a Major Fund Family

The websites of Vanguard, Fidelity, and T. Rowe Price make it easy to find information on index fund characteristics and performance and to open an account. So do the sites of other fund families.

Step 4. Select Your Investments

Depending on your asset allocation, you will invest in low management fee stock and bond index funds from the fund family you choose. Generally, this means a U.S. total stock index fund, a broad international stock index fund, and a U.S. bond index fund. The proportion in stocks should be 70% in the U.S. stock index fund and 30% in the international stock index fund.

Step 5. Rebalance Your Portfolio

Different funds in your portfolio will grow at different rates, so to maintain your asset allocation you will need to occasionally rebalance your portfolio. Every six months, check your investments or speak with your adviser about the need to rebalance— or buy a target retirement date fund, and let the fund manager do the rebalancing.

Tips on Investing

- **Avoid active fund management.** The proposition that active fund managers can—in return for their fees—beat the market and boost your returns over those of index funds is an investment industry con game.

- **Leave it to the markets.** U.S. and global companies will continue to grow over the long term, and you will share in that growth if you let the highly efficient markets do their work.

- **Plan withdrawals carefully.** As the time to start living on your retirement income approaches, carefully consider the income sources you will rely on, the portion you will withdraw, and which investments you'll withdraw from. Avoid aggressive withdrawals in the early years of retirement.

- **Plan your legacy.** Prepare a will and a trust agreement that minimizes taxes while securing the financial future of your heirs, as appropriate to their needs. Consider appointing a directed trustee and instructing them to continue to invest in a balanced portfolio of low management fee index funds.

What's the Point?

Intelligent investing is simple and easy to implement. Just ignore the investment pros and invest in a globally diversified portfolio of low management fee index funds in an asset allocation appropriate for you.

CHAPTER 46

Bulletproof Your Plan

**There are a million ways to screw things up, but, fortunately,
just a few ways to get them right.**
—Anonymous

People often make mistakes when they turn simple projects into complicated ones. Intelligent financial planning is really simple. Here are my final tips. They work for me and my clients. You won't go wrong if you follow them.

You Won't Go Wrong If You . . .

- Set financial goals, and track your progress. Spend less than you earn, and save the difference.

- Pay as you go, and stay out of debt.

- Pay your mortgage off early and be a real homeowner.

- Be as wise with insurance as insurers are with their risks.

- Avoid special-offer interest rates and free meals from financial firms.

- Invest in index funds, allocate your assets, and periodically rebalance.

- Remain calm during times of bad news and market volatility.

- Avoid people with scare stories, market-beating returns, and sophisticated products.

- Build a small team of advisers you trust—and pay for their advice.

- Face money problems as they arise, get the facts, and take action.

- Plan retirement well in advance, so you're prepared for old age.

What's the Point?

Empower yourself. Take control of your financial life. To be in the top
1% of Americans, you have to be 10 times as diligent as others.
Fortunately, this is not difficult.

PART TWELVE

Sources, Support, and Supplemental Reading

The suggestions in this book often contradict those that you will find in many other sources. I've draw from sources with expertise *and* objectivity—and made every effort to rely on data and facts as opposed to opinion and musings. When I've relied on opinion, I've focused on sources of objective expert opinion to the greatest extent possible.

This part compiles those sources by chapter and points to others. It also suggests supplemental reading you can do if you want or need to delve deeper into any area.

CHAPTER 47

How Can You Know?

Trust, but verify.
—President Ronald Reagan

Introduction: Reversal of Fortune

The statistics on assets come from the U.S. Internal Revenue Service, Statistics of Income Division "SOI Data Tables," July 2008 (www.census.gov/compendia/statab/2011/tables/11s0718.pdf).

For the paper showing how financially fragile most Americans are, see Annamaria Lusardi, Daniel J. Schneider, and Peter Tufano, "Financially Fragile Household: Evidence and Implications," The National Bureau of Economic Research, May 2011 (http://papers .nber.org/papers/w17072).

In general, U.S. Census data on income can help you place your own level of income, assets, debt, and net worth in context. However, whenever possible, consult state-level data because these statistics vary by region.

Chapter 1: Bad Things Happen to Good People

The sagging fortunes of the middle class have been well documented, most accurately in U.S. Census income figures compiled since the 1970s, which show a steady decline. The quote leading off this chapter is from the *New York Times* Economix blog: "The

Sagging of the Middle Class," June 14, 2010 (http://economix
.blogs.nytimes.com/2010/06/14/the-sagging-of-the-middle-class/
?scp=12&sq=middle%20class%20decline&st=cse).

Paul Johnston's case is real, but his name and other details have
been changed to protect his privacy.

As millions of people fell out of the middle class in the recession of 2008–2009, they made unprecedented use of unemployment insurance and food stamps. The one-in-eight figure is from
the *New York Times* article "Food Stamp Use Soars, and Stigma
Fades" by Jason DeParle and Robert Gebeloff, November 28, 2009
(www.nytimes.com/2009/11/29/us/29foodstamps.html).

Foreclosures also reached post–Great Depression records during
the 2008–2009 recession. RealtyTrac (www.realtytrac.com) reports
U.S. and state-level data on foreclosures and provides related learning resources. The March 2010 statistic is from the article "Rising
Foreclosures Reverberate Across Economy," posted by Karen Datko
on MSN Money, July 29, 2010 (http://articles.moneycentral.msn
.com/Banking/HomeFinancing/article.aspx?post=1787497).

The recession also reduced retirement savings by baby boomers as evidenced by the statistic in this chapter from *Retirement
Income* blog: "Average Retirement Savings: All Measurements
Lead to the Same Conclusion" (www.retirement-income.net/
blog/2008/08/14/average-retirement-savings-all-measurements
-lead-to-the-same-conclusion).

Chapter 2: Lifestyles of the Broke and Homeless
Soccer great George Best's quote is from "George Best, Soccer
Star and Pop Icon, Is Dead at 59" by Jack Bell, in the *New York
Times*, November 26, 2005 (www.nytimes.com/2005/11/26/sports/
soccer/26best.html?scp=2&sq=%22George%20Best%22&st=cse).

The table was calculated from data from the Bureau of Economic Analysis National Income & Product Accounts, Table 5.1, "Saving and Investment by Sector," periodically revised (www .bea.gov/national/nipaweb/TableView.asp?SelectedTable=137& ViewSeries=NO&Java=no&Request3Place=N&3Place=N&FromView =YES&Freq=Year&FirstYear=1960&LastYear=2009&3Place =N&Update=UpdateJavaBox=no).

The boom of the mid-2000s was fueled largely by debt, as reported in articles like the one quoted here: "Consumer Debt Avalanche Ready to Roll in 2009: Is There Any Help?" by Naomi Monk, January 3, 2009 (www.smallcommercialmortgageonline.com/blog/2009/01/ 03/consumer-debt-avalanche-ready-to-roll-in-2009-is-there-any -help). As noted, stagnant incomes could not finance the boom, so consumers—abetted by the credit card, mortgage lending, and auto loan and leasing industries—racked up record levels of debt. This left them extremely vulnerable to the effects of the economic downturn.

I recommend you read the source of this quote by Charles Hugh Smith: "Dear 'Middle Class' Americans: Most of You Are Debt Serfs with Zero Assets," at *Business Insider* (www.businessinsider .com/dear-middle-class-americans-most-of-you-are-debt-serfs -with-zero-assets-2010-10). It's a scathing indictment of the high-consumption lifestyle.

China's economic accomplishments have been well documented, and that nation has committed itself to economic growth. Although China may make mistakes in managing its largely government-directed economy, that economy has passed Japan as the second largest. It bears repeating that China, a developing economy, holds about $1 trillion of U.S. debt. The statistic here on China's saving rate is from the Bank for International Settlements Working Paper 312, "China's High Saving Rate: Myth and Reality" by Guonan Ma and Wang Yi, June 2010 (www.bis.org/publ/ work312.pdf?noframes=1).

Chapter 3: What Marshmallows Can Teach You About Money

Walter Mischel's "marshmallow study" with children has been widely reported on and at times debated. Here I am relying on the most recent diligent (and accessible) inquiry into Mischel's work that I could find, which was Jonah Lehrer's article "Don't! The Secret of Self-Control" in the *New Yorker*, May 18, 2009 (www.newyorker .com/reporting/2009/05/18/090518fa_fact_lehrer).

Criticisms of his work usually state that healthy and successful living is the result of far more factors than delayed gratification, particularly as exhibited by children in the circumstances that Mischel creates. Nevertheless, the key skill in saving money and avoiding debt is clearly the ability to delay gratification in the form of current consumption.

Chapter 4: A Map Won't Help Without a Destination

The question of whether a million dollars is what it used to be is easily answered: It isn't. However, the point here is that $1 million invested to produce an annual return of even 5% will produce the 2009 annual median income for U.S. households. So, a million is still a decent sum. My source for the income data is *Income, Poverty and Health Insurance Coverage in the United States: 2009*, U.S. Census Bureau, September 2010, p. 5, Table 1, "Income and Earning Summary Measures by Selected Characteristics, 2008 and 2009." This table shows the Median Income Estimate for All Households as $49,777 for 2009.

Chapter 5: Focus on Your Net Worth

The nonprofit Corporation for Enterprise Development (CFED) (http://cfed.org), the source of the quotation that opens this chapter, works to promote financial literacy among households as well as policies and programs designed to alleviate poverty. CFED's 2009–2010 Assets & Opportunities Scorecard (http://scorecard

.cfed.org) provides interesting, state-by-state data on households' financial status.

Chapter 6: The Thrill of a Budget Beats the Agony of Poverty

Reducing spending is far less difficult than people imagine before they actually do it. As Ramit Sethi points out in his August 17, 2009, *MintLife* article "How to Save More Money by Doing Less" (www.mint.com/blog/saving/save-more-money-by-doing-less), many people don't know where 20% to 30% of their money goes. Once you know where it goes, you can start deciding whether those expenditures are worthwhile or wasted money.

The sample budgets were developed by Scott Shires of Shires Financial Group Inc., Aurora, Colorado.

Chapter 7: Pay Yourself First

"Pay yourself first" is great advice that many people find hard to follow. As financial adviser Jim Lentini of Lentini Insurance & Investments Inc. points out in a July 20, 2010, article "You and Your Retirement Strategy" in the *Santa Clarita Valley Signal* (www.the -signal.com/archives/31199), systematic savings is the way to build a retirement fund. And the best way to systematize savings is through automatic monthly or bimonthly transfers.

Chapter 8: Build Savings Muscle

College student Ashton McDonald has solid ideas for controlling expenses in his article "7 Tips to Reduce Living Expenses" (http://helium.com/items/1867281-tips-for-reducing-living -expenses). This article focuses on reducing overall living expenses, wisely counseling that we should distinguish wants from needs. He also recommends controlling spending on utilities and entertainment, two areas that can increase your "monetary metabolism" while you're not looking.

Apart from supplying me with a useful metaphor, *The Abs Diet* by David Zinczenko (Rodale, 2004) presents a no-nonsense system for reducing physical flab.

Chapter 9: Don't Abet Debt

Though many people acted as if the housing bust and subsequent recession of the 2000s was unpredictable, some observers expressed concern over the levels of debt that consumers were racking up before the bust. Among them was Johns Hopkins University economist Christopher D. Carroll, quoted here in 2007 in "The Consumer Crunch" by Michael Mandel, in *Business Week*, November 26, 2007 (www.businessweek.com/magazine/content/07_48/b4060001.htm).

Chapter 10: Debt Out!

Although most Americans decided to reduce their debt during and after the recession, the portrait of debtors provided in "Given a Shovel, Americans Dig Deeper into Debt" by Gretchen Morgenson in the *New York Times*, July 20, 2008, is truly frightening (www.nytimes.com/2008/07/20/business/20debt.html#). It's equally scary that the reporter is correct in stating that Diane was "was a dream customer for lenders" in that she willingly devoted a staggering proportion of her income to interest and fees, until she could no longer handle it.

Incidentally, Morgenson's reporting on the debt and mortgage crisis and on financial institutions' role in it—and, subsequently, on the lack of serious financial reform—provides a valuable "first draft of history" of the financial crisis and recession of the late 2000s. Check out the archives at www.nytimes.com.

Chapter 11: The Nuclear Debt Option

As the press release quoted here states, bankruptcy filings actually increased despite 2005 legislation designed to make bankruptcy more difficult. "Consumer Bankruptcy Filings Increase 9 Percent in 2010," American Bankruptcy Institute, press release, January 3, 2011 (www.abiworld.org/AM/Template.cfm?Section =Home&TEMPLATE=/CM/ContentDisplay.cfm&CONTENTID =62756).

That same press release notes that "Annual consumer filings have increased each year since the Bankruptcy Abuse Prevention and Consumer Protection Act was enacted in 2005." Including the term *consumer protection* in legislation designed to make it more difficult for consumers to legally get out from under debt reveals Congress's priorities as well as a grim sense of humor.

The bankruptcy statistics quoted here from "Annual Business and Non-Business Filings by Year (1980–2009)" by the American Bankruptcy Institute (www.abiworld.org/AM/AMTemplate.cfm ?Section=Home&CONTENTID=60229&TEMPLATE=/CM/ ContentDisplay.cfm) are truly remarkable. From 2006 through 2010, consumer bankruptcies averaged *1 million per year*. The single surest way to avoid bankruptcy is to avoid debt.

Chapter 12: Edit Your Credit

John Ulzheimer, president of consumer education at Smart Credit.com, is a wellspring of information on the wise use of credit and the ins and outs of credit reporting and scoring. This quote, from his July 14, 2010, *MintLife* article "Deciphering FICO: More Than a Third of Scores Now Under 650" (www.mint.com/blog/ trends/deciphering-fico-more-than-a-third-of-scores-now-under -650), only adds to the evidence I've presented in Part Three that the 2000s debt explosion had many ill effects.

Chapter 13: Investing in Your Home

As a purely financial investment, stocks far outperform real estate, as evidenced by this quote from "Real Estate vs. Stocks" by

Sara Clemence, writing at Forbes.com on May 27, 2005 (www
.forbes.com/2005/05/27/cx_sc_0527home.html). Comparisons of
stocks and housing as investments are clouded by factors I discuss
in this chapter, not the least of which is the strong emotional
appeal of homeownership among Americans.

I am not saying that dedicated real estate investors fail to
become independently wealthy. Rather, I suggest that the approach
to investing in stocks presented in this book is a far surer (and easier) path to wealth for most people than real estate investing or,
more to the point, than relying on your primary residence as the
key asset in your wealth-building plan.

Over relatively short terms, housing can and does outperform
stocks, as stated in "Stocks Versus Real Estate" by *Money Magazine*
senior editor Marlys Harris, quoted by CNNMoney.com on July 4,
2007 (http://money.cnn.com/galleries/2007/real_estate/0704/gallery
.stocks_v_realestate.moneymag/index.html).

The S&P/Case-Shiller Home Price Index (www.standardand
poors.com/indices/sp-case-shiller-home-price-indices/en/us/
?indexId=spusa-cashpidff--p-us----) is widely recognized as providing reliable data on U.S. home prices.

Chapter 14: Home Economics: Should You Buy or Rent?

The white paper quoted here, *Reforming America's Housing Finance
Market: A Report to Congress* from February 2011 by the Department
of the Treasury and Department of Housing and Urban Development, is a remarkable document (www.treasury.gov/initiatives/
Documents/Reforming%20America%27s%20Housing%20Finance
%20Market.pdf).

While a white paper is a far cry from legislation, the policy priorities that the document describes might surprise some readers.
Those priorities include "reducing government support of housing
finance and winding down Fannie Mae and Freddie Mac on a

responsible timetable," as well as increased protection for consumers and "increased transparency, standardization, and accountability in the securitization chain."

The August 23, 2010, article quoting the Harris Interactive survey "Will Growing Rental Trends Undermine U.S. Home Sales?" by Keith Jurow appeared on the World Property Channel (www.worldpropertychannel.com/us-markets/residential-real-estate-1/real-estate-news-rent-versus-buy-a-home-david-neithercut-equity-residential-wall-street-journal-homes-for-rent-condos-for-rent-national-apartment-association-3040.php).

Rules of thumb like the price to rent ratio help, but major financial decisions such as home buying (and career choice) are too complex and personal to boil down to formulas. As indicated by the title of the article from which the quote about the ratio is drawn—"In a Sour Home Market, Buying Often Beats Renting" by David Loenhardt, *New York Times*, April 21, 2010 (www.nytimes.com/2010/04/21/business/economy/21leonhardt.html?_r=1)—it depends on the market as well as on personal factors such as income, timing, and your need for space.

Nonetheless, I offer guidelines on affordability in this chapter. The income data are drawn from "Median U.S. Household Income by State" by U.S. News Staff, *U.S. News and World Report*, October 5, 2010 (www.usnews.com/opinion/articles/2010/10/05/median-us-household-income-by-state_print.html).

Chapter 15: Foreclosures and Short Sales

The opening quote is from a February 5, 2011, *New York Times* article "Housing Bubbles Are Few and Far Between" by Robert J. Shiller (www.nytimes.com/2011/02/06/business/06view.html). Shiller is an economist, author, and professor at Yale University.

The figure from CoreLogic for underwater homes is from the March 8, 2011, *Huffington Post* article "Number of Underwater

Mortgages Rises as More Homeowners Fall Behind" by Derek Kravitz (www.huffingtonpost.com/2011/03/08/number-of-underwater -mort_n_833000.html). The 11.1 million homes underwater were as of October to December 2010, indicating that the housing bust will be with us for a very long time.

Florida-based real estate attorney Antonio Faga generously provided guidance and material for this chapter in an interview on February 22, 2011. As Faga points out, you can make money in foreclosures but they are not for everyone. Short sales are not as complex, but you have to be the right kind of buyer and have knowledgeable advisers who are representing you.

Chapter 16: Outliving Your Mortgage

The source of the statistics leading off this chapter is the *2009 American Housing Survey*, U.S. Census Bureau, Table 3-15. Mortgage Characteristics—Owner-Occupied Units (www.census.gov/ hhes/www/housing/ahs/ahs09/3-15.xls). The survey itself, like much of the data on household finances from the U.S. Census Bureau, contains some startling information. Considering that all seniors with mortgages have a median of 14 years left on their payments, even if they were all 65 and all had the median time remaining on their mortgages, they would be making payments until they were almost 80.

The major benefit of owning over renting your home should be actually owning it. Living in a paid-off house or condo and facing nothing but (reasonable) property taxes and home maintenance costs is not a bad deal. But it happens only if you pay off your mortgage.

The Money-Zine mortgage calculator referred to in this chapter can be found at www.money-zine.com/Calculators/Mortgage -Calculators/Mortgage-Amortization-Table.

Chapter 17: The Term of Your Life

The statistics on life insurance are from "Facts About Life 2010," September 2010, issued by LIMRA International Inc. (formerly the Life Insurance and Market Research Association) (www.limra .com/NewsCenter/FactsFAQs/Default.aspx?Lang=EN& Region=NA).

For more information on term life insurance and calculating your insurance needs, see insurance agent Linda Rey's June 17, 2010, article "Term Life Insurance: Getting the Best Deal on the Term Coverage You Need" at *Equifax Finance Blog* (http://insur ance.equifax.com/search/label/term%20life%20insurance).

Chapter 18: Cash Value Life Insurance

Fee-only insurance consultant, Scott J. Witt of Milwaukee- based Witt Actuarial Services (http://wittactuarialservices.com) generously provided guidance for material in this chapter in an in-depth interview on March 2, 2011.

There are very few fee-only insurance consultants relative to other types of financial advisers. A partial list, from the website of New York–based fee-only insurance adviser Glenn Daily (www .glenndaily.com), includes David Barkhausen in Illinois (www.life insuranceadvisorsinc.com), Patrick Collins in California (www .schultzcollins.com), James Hunt in New Hampshire (www.evaluate lifeinsurance.org), Peter Katt in Michigan (www.peterkatt.com), JJ MacNab in Maryland (www.deathandtaxes.com), and Richard M. Weber in California (www.ethicaledgeconsulting.com).

Paying a fee-only adviser to evaluate your insurance needs will give you more objective advice than relying on commissioned agents and salespeople. Fee-only insurance advisers derive none of their income from commissions from (or referrals to) insurance companies, agents, or salespeople. In addition to providing objective advice, they can design policies to be underwritten by an insurer that meet your goals in more economical ways than standard policies, which build in high commissions and features that often add cost without adding much value.

Chapter 19: Annuities: Don't Toss the Baby Out with the Bathwater

Critics of annuities and the practices that are used to sell them include Barbara Roper, director of investor protection at the Consumer Federation of America (CFA) as quoted in the article "Annuity Tax Alteration May Hurt Middle Class," March 7, 2011 (www .sheryljmoore.com/2011/03/annuity-tax-alteration-may-hurt -middle-class).

In response to a proposed amendment to the financial regulatory reform bill that made its way through Congress in 2010, Roper stated that "It [the amendment] paints a target on the backs of senior Americans who are most likely to be targeted with abusive variable annuity sales practices," according to a CFA press release dated May 13, 2010.

Roper has also said that "Salespeople typically downplay the complexity of indexed annuities and their long lock-up periods" in a *Bloomberg Investment News* piece titled "Indexed Annuities 'Terrible Ideas' for Seniors, Says Wharton Prof" (www.investment news.com/article/20110124/FREE/110129973). The Wharton professor referenced is Kent Smetters, a professor of insurance at University of Pennsylvania's Wharton School.

The Smartmoney.com report was "Annuities for Retirement: The Best, and the Rest" by Elizabeth O'Brien and Matthew Heimer on April 7, 2010 (www.smartmoney.com/retirement/planning/ Annuities-for-Retirement-The-Best-and-the-Rest/?zone=intromes sage).

Chapter 20: Health Insurance

The survey on satisfaction was reported in the July 30, 2010, article "On Medicare's 45th Anniversary, 85% of Retirees Are 'Very' or 'Somewhat' Satisfied with Their Medicare Coverage" by ExtendHealth (https://www.extendhealth.com/about/press-center/medicare-anniversary-satisfaction-with-coverage).

Healthcare reform as enacted by Congress and signed by the president in 2010 (and fiercely debated before and since) is being phased in. One of the most lucid explanations I've seen of the legislation's provisions is "Health Care Reform Bill Explained in Simple Terms" by Robin Stark-Humphrey (www.associatedcontent.com/article/2872454/health_care_reform_bill_explained_in.html?cat=5).

For details on COBRA, access the U.S. Department of Labor's information on the subject (www.dol.gov/ebsa/newsroom/fscobra.html).

In regard to high-deductible health plans and health savings accounts, see the U.S. Treasury Publication No. 969 "Health Savings Accounts and Other Tax-Favored Health Plans" (www.irs.gov/pub/irs-pdf/p969.pdf). Also see the May 29, 2009, *New York Times* article "The Many Hidden Costs of High-Deductible Health Insurance" by Walecia Konrad (www.nytimes.com/2009/05/30/health/30patient.html).

Chapter 21: Goldman Sachs: Paragon or Pariah?

The quote opening this chapter is from "Blankfein Flunks Asset Management as Clark Vows No More Goldman" by Richard Teitelbaum, January 24, 2011 (www.bloomberg.com/news/2011-01-25/blankfein-flunks-asset-management-as-jim-clark-vows-no-more-goldman-sachs.html).

Morningstar (www.morningstar.com) is an independent investment research company well known for tracking mutual fund performance, which was the company's initial focus. Morningstar now provides research on a wide range of investments as well as portfolio tools.

The "great vampire squid" quote is from the article "The Great American Bubble Machine" by Matt Taibbi in the April 5, 2010, issue of *Rolling Stone* (www.rollingstone.com/politics/news/the -great-american-bubble-machine-20100405).

The effects of investment banks converting from partnerships to corporations is nicely documented by Michael Lewis in his article "The End" in the November 11, 2008, issue of *Portfolio* (www .portfolio.com/news-markets/national-news/portfolio/2008/11/ 11/The-End-of-Wall-Streets-Boom).

In another vein, Lewis points out, "To this day, the willingness of a Wall Street investment bank to pay me hundreds of thousands of dollars to dispense investment advice to grownups remains a mystery to me. I was 24 years old, with no experience of, or particular interest in, guessing which stocks and bonds would rise and which would fall." Things have not changed on the Street since then, nor since Lewis wrote *Liar's Poker*, his bestseller based on his experiences at Salomon Brothers.

The figures on advertising are from a press release titled "Kantar Media Reports U.S. Advertising Expenditures Increased 6.5 Percent in 2010," dated March 17, 2011 (http://kantarmediana.com/intelli gence/press/us-advertising-expenditures-increased-65-percent -2010). Kantar Media tracks and analyzes worldwide print, radio, TV, Internet, cinema, mobile, social media, and outdoor advertising.

See the Index Funds Advisors site (www.ifa.com) and the Dimensional Fund Advisors site (www.dfaus.com) for studies on the failure of active funds to outperform the markets. At the Index Funds Advisors site, click the "Articles," "Archives," and "Books" tabs for information. At the Dimensional Fund Advisors site, click on "Library" for articles. One especially good one at the Dimensional site is "The Informational Efficiency of Stock Prices: A Review" by James L. Davis, which reviews various studies of fund performance along the dimensions of sample size, benchmarks, and selection bias to reveal the ways in which some studies have inaccurately shown active management in a more favorable light than passive management.

Chapter 22: The Fix Is (Still) In

The opening quote is from *Wall Street: A History* by Charles R. Geisst (Oxford University Press, 1997), a well-researched, highly readable history of Wall Street. As Geisst makes clear, Wall Street has a long tradition of shearing sheep while presenting itself as standard-bearer of capitalism. His book ends with the industry lobbying for repeal of the Glass-Steagall Act, which separated commercial banking and investment banking in 1933. Glass-Steagall was repealed in 1999 by the Gramm-Leach-Bliley Act.

Many observers have commented on the lack of mortgage relief for distressed homeowners. On November 6, 2008, in *WSJ Real Time Economics*, John Kocjan, head of Deloitte Consulting financial services practice, said, "As recently as Wednesday, the Treasury and the Federal Deposit Insurance Corp. has proposed a plan to guarantee the mortgages of up to 3 million homeowners. And FDIC Chairman Sheila Bair told the Senate Banking Committee, 'There has been some progress—but it's not been enough, and we need to act quickly and we need to act dramatically.'" "Guest Post: Quickly Building 'Industrial Strength' Homeowner Relief" (http://blogs .wsj.com/economics/2008/11/06/guest-post-quickly-building -industrial-strength-homeowner-relief).

The action Bair called for never materialized, as evidenced by 3 million foreclosures in 2009 (http://money.cnn.com/2010/01/14/ real_estate/record_foreclosure_year) and almost 2 million in 2010 (www.wsws.org/articles/2010/dec2010/fore-d31.shtml).

In the 2002 Berkshire Hathaway Annual Report, Warren Buffett said, "I view derivatives as time bombs, both for the parties that deal in them and the economic system." He closed this section of the annual report by saying, "In my view, derivatives are financial weapons of mass destruction, carrying dangers that, while now latent, are potentially lethal" (www.berkshirehathaway.com/letters/2002pdf.pdf).

See my blog post "Rich and Poor Serve Their Wall Street Masters," January 25, 2010, at *Huffington Post* for more details on how FINRA favors the industry over investors (http://huffingtonpost .com/dan-solin/rich-and-poor-serve-their_b_812718.html).

The numbers quoted on FINRA awards in 2005 and 2009 are from "FINRA Enforcement Activity (Exhibit)," Reuters Graphics/ Stephen Culp (http://graphics.thomsonreuters.com/11/02/US _FINRA0211_SC.gif).

Nobel Prize–winning, Princeton University economist Paul Krugman has often railed against the lack of meaningful reform after the financial crisis in his *New York Times* op-ed columns. On March 3, 2009, in an article titled "Zombie Financial Ideas" (http:// krugman.blogs.nytimes.com/2009/03/03/zombie-financial-ideas), Krugman said, "Every plan we've heard from the Treasury amounts to the same thing—an attempt to socialize the losses while privatizing the gains [of the financial services industry]."

Chapter 23: Wall Street's Casinos

The opening quote from Jim Cramer is typical of stock and fund pickers who admit deep fallibility while implying that they have knowledge that can make you money. (The quote is from www.woopidoo.com/business_quotes/authors/jim-cramer/ index.htm.) In fairness to Cramer, and as his show *Mad Money* amply demonstrates, he is an entertainer and not to be taken seriously as a guide to financial matters. This is particularly the case after he recommended Lehman Brothers at $55.18 a share on October 17, 2005, only to see it fall to $16 a share on September 5, 2008, when he it called it a "screaming buy" (http://2parse.com/?p =2312). Lehman went bankrupt in 2009.

Run for the hills if an investment firm has labeled you "a sophisticated investor" is excellent advice from the article "Can You Afford Sophistication?" at Index Funds Advisors (www.ifa.com/emailcampaign/QOW/Can_You_Afford_Sophistication.aspx).

Goldman Sachs used the fact that its customers were sophisticated investors as an argument against regulation and as an excuse for practices, such as not disclosing its position in investments it sells. As Thomas Frank details in "Goldman and the Sophisticated Investor," when everyone is "sophisticated," "everything is permitted" (http://online.wsj.com/article/NA_WSJ_PUB :SB10001424052748703866704575224511672855990.html [subscription required]).

Also, be aware that, at many investment firms, the term *sophisticated investor* also means "high net worth individual" or, in more common parlance, a major sales prospect for "exotic" investments (meaning investments that stand a good chance of being profitable for the house and losers for the investor).

Chapter 24: Advice About Advisers

If you're looking for an adviser, the websites of the organizations mentioned in this chapter are good starting points:

National Association of Professional Advisers: www.napfa.org

Dimensional Fund Advisors: www.dfaus.com

Center for Fiduciary Studies: www.fi360.com

However, notwithstanding the recommendations of these sources or others, I strongly recommend using advisers who focus on your asset allocation and who recommend a globally diversified portfolio consisting *only* of low management fee index funds, passively managed funds, or exchange traded funds.

Chapter 25: Don't Just Do Something—Stand There

The opening quotation is from the article "Random Walks in Stock Market Prices" by Eugene F. Fama, *Financial Analysts Journal*, September–October 1965 (reprinted January–February 1995). It still stands up well. The securities markets are even more efficient now, due to the speed at which financial information and news that may affect the prices of securities is disseminated.

For some perspective on Fama, see the June 1, 1999, interview with him at the Index Funds Advisors site (www.ifa.com/Articles/ Interview_with_Eugene_Fama.aspx).

The literature on the efficiency of the stock market is broad, deep, objective, and academically sound. Again, I refer you to the library at www.dfaus.com and the articles and books at www.ifa .com. I discuss the research of Fama and his coauthor on my projects, Kenneth French, in *The Smartest Portfolio You'll Ever Own*. Fama and French have been called "the smartest people alive in finance" (among others). Also see "How the Really Smart Money Invests" by Shawn Tully, *Fortune Magazine*, July 6, 1998.

Chapter 26: May the (Market) Force Be with You

The core of these examples is from "3 April Fools Investment Tricks" by Allan S. Roth, founder of Wealth Logic, author of the excellent book *How a Second Grader Beats Wall Street* (Wiley, 2005), and contributor at CBS MoneyWatch.com blog (http://money watch.bnet.com/investing/blog/irrational-investor/3-april -fools-investment-tricks/3079).

Chapter 27: Why Index Funds Work for Investors

The opening quotation is from the article "The Efficient Market Hypothesis and the Random Walk Theory" by Gary Karz at *Investor Home*, which offers additional perspectives on the efficient market theory (http://investorhome.com/emh.htm).

Chapter 28: The Risk-Return Tradeoff

The opening quotation for this chapter is from Charles Tremper at UCLA (http://thinkexist.com/quotations/risk/2.html).

The risk-based allocations in this chapter are consistent with those in my book *The Smartest Portfolio You'll Ever Own* (Perigee, 2011).

Chapter 29: Assessing Your Risk Capacity

The opening quote is from "An Experimental Study of Risk-Taking" by John Steiner, Institute of Psychiatry, De Crespigny Park, Denmark Hill, London, published in abridged form in the *Proceedings of the Royal Society of Medicine*, December 1970 (www.ncbi.nlm.nih.gov/pmc/articles/PMC1812382/pdf/procrsmed00288-0083.pdf).

The story of lottery players Ray Otero and Richie Randazzo is from "Thousands Later, He Sees Lottery's Cruelty Up Close" by Alan Feuer, *New York Times*, August 21, 2008 (www.nytimes.com/2008/08/22/nyregion/22super.html). I include it as a cautionary tale for investors. The nature of the markets, coupled with the ways in which investing has so often been portrayed in the popular and business press, causes many investors to confuse investing and gambling.

I highly recommend Jason Zweig's October 1, 2002, *Money* magazine article "Are You Wired for Wealth?" (http://money.cnn.com/magazines/moneymag/moneymag_archive/2002/10/01/328637/index.htm). It's an excellent summary of the parallels between gambling and hyperactive investing. The Index Funds Advisors site draws similar parallels in the article "Active Investors Are Gamblers" (www.ifa.com/12steps/step1/step1page2.asp).

Books to read to increase your knowledge of investing include the following:

Bernstein, William. *The Intelligent Asset Allocator*. New York: McGraw-Hill Professional, 2000.

Bogle, John C. *The Little Book of Common Sense Investing*. Hoboken, NJ: Wiley, 2007.

Burton, Malkiel G. *A Random Walk Down Wall Street*. New York: Norton, 1973.

Hebner, Mark T. *Index Funds: The 12-Step Program for Active Investors*. Irvine, CA: Index Funds Advisors, 2006.

Larimore, Taylor, Mel Lindauer, and Michael LeBoeuf. *The Boglehead's Guide to Investing*. Hoboken, NJ: Wiley, 2007.

Chapter 30: Fighting the Worst Enemies of High Returns

John C. Bogle founded the Vanguard mutual fund family in 1974. In 1975, he launched the Vanguard 500 Index Fund, which was the first index fund available to individual investors. Now retired from Vanguard, Bogle is the author of a wonderful guide to wealth building called *The Little Book of Common Sense Investing*. Also see *The Boglehead's Guide to Investing* by Taylor Larimore, Mel Lindauer, and Michael LeBoeuf.

The study comparing the performance of proprietary funds to similar funds managed by nonbrokerage-related fund families was based on data by Lipper Inc. initially reported at http://moneycentral.msn.com/content/p27026.asp. It is no longer available online.

"Mutual Fund Objective Misclassification" is the study of the Morningstar funds by Moon Kim, Ravi Shukla, and Michael Thomas, published in the July–August 2000 issue of the *Journal of*

Economics and Business and reviewed in Larry E. Swedroe's book *Rational Investing in Irrational Times.*

Chapter 31: The Simple Logic of Asset Allocation

Berkshire Hathaway CEO Warren Buffett has long been a proponent of index funds. This quote from the company's 2004 annual report is just one instance when the Oracle of Omaha has extolled the virtues of index funds, although he is often wrongfully held up as an exemplar of stock picking.

The article "Does Asset Allocation Policy Explain 40, 90, or 100 Percent of Performance?" by Roger G. Ibbotson and Paul D. Kaplan analyzed how much of portfolio performance—defined as total returns—is explained by asset allocation policy (http://corporate .morningstar.com/ib/documents/MethodologyDocuments/IBB Associates/AssetAllocationExplain.pdf). The authors concluded that 90% of the variability of returns *over time*, 100% of the *level* of returns, and 40% of the variability of returns among funds is explained by asset allocation policy.

The article "Explaining Stock Returns: A Literature Survey" by James L. Davis provides an excellent overview of the academic research on the causes of variance in the returns produced by investments in stocks (www.dfaus.com/2009/05/explaining-stock -returns-a-literature-survey.html).

I strongly recommend that you complete the Risk Capacity Survey at www.smartestinvestmentbook.com. It will help you determine your asset allocation.

Chapter 32: A Simple Way to Implement Your Investing Plan

Jonathan Clements, the source of the quotation that opens this chapter, was the personal finance columnist for the *Wall Street*

Journal for 18 years and is the author of *The Little Book of Main Street Money* (Wiley, 2009). I highly recommend this book.

For anyone getting into investing (or for seasoned investors—particularly hyperactive ones), I strongly recommend Mark Hebner's book *Index Funds: The 12-Step Program for Active Investors.* Mark is the president of Index Funds Advisors Inc., with which I am affiliated.

Chapter 33: How Much Will You Need?

The figures from the Employee Benefits Research Institute are from the MSN Money article "What's Your Magic Number for Retirement?" by Bankrate.com (http://articles.moneycentral.msn .com/RetirementandWills/CreateaPlan/WhatsYourMagic NumberForRetirement.aspx).

Boston University economics professor Laurence Kotlikoff sees a dim future for Social Security and was a vocal critic of the U.S. debt situation in his book (with Scott Burns) *The Coming Generational Storm* (MIT Press, 2005). In their subsequent book, *Spend 'Til the End: Raising Your Living Standard in Today's Economy and When You Retire* (Simon & Schuster, 2010), they bring things down to the more personal level.

Chapter 34: Beating the 401(k) Rip-Off

The opening quotation is from the article "Retirement Rip-Off" by Neil Weinberg, posted on December 11, 2006, on Forbes.com. I recommend this article for its coverage of the problems with 401(k) plans and its reporting on suits brought against companies that have used 401(k) plans for their own profit at the expense of their employees (www.forbes.com/forbes/2006/1211/135.html).

I discuss the many problems with 401(k), 403(b), and 457(b) plans in *The Smartest 401(k) Book You'll Ever Read* (Perigee, 2008).

These plans represent a truly sad (yet wildly successful) scheme by the financial services industry to enrich themselves at the expense of working Americans.

Chapter 35: Making Your Money Outlive You

The opening quotation is from the April 25, 2011, article "Americans Raiding Retirement Funds Early" by Sheyna Steiner on Bankrate.com (www.bankrate.com/finance/consumer-index/april-2011-raiding-retirement-fund.aspx#ixzz1NBjKNGz2).

For facts on Americans' (lack of) preparation for retirement, see the January 5, 2011, article, "16 Statistics About the Coming Retirement Crisis That Will Drop Your Jaw" by Michael Snyder at *Business Insider* (www.businessinsider.com/facts-about-retirement-crisis-2010-12). Another survey cited by this blog states that "24 percent of U.S. workers have postponed their planned retirement age at least once during the past year."

Data in the table come from Social Security Online (www.socialsecurity.gov) Actuarial Publications Period Life Table (www.ssa.gov/OACT/STATS/table4c6.html).

Peter Lynch was the very successful manager of the Magellan Fund, a flagship fund at Fidelity.

William Bernstein is the author of *The Four Pillars of Investing* (McGraw-Hill, 2010), among other excellent books.

William Bengen is an icon of withdrawal research who created the 4% withdrawal rule and the floor-and-ceiling approach in an effort to guide retirees toward safe withdrawal rates. Also, see Bob's Financial Website (http://bobsfinancialwebsite.com/Variable Withdrawals.html#Bengen) for a variety of withdrawal strategies created by financial theorists.

For more information on managing your money in retirement, also see my book *The Smartest Retirement Book You'll Ever Read.*

Chapter 36: Sources of Cash in Retirement

The average Social Security retirement income figure of $1,176 in 2010 is from the Social Security Administration Office of Retirement and Disability Policy publication "Fast Facts & Figures About Social Security, 2011" (www.ssa.gov/policy/docs/chartbooks/fast _facts/2011/fast_facts11.html).

You can estimate your Social Security benefit, based on your actual data, using the Benefit Calculator at www.socialsecurity .gov/estimator.

The 660,000 figure for reverse mortgages is from the February 11, 2011, AARP article "10 Things You Should Know About Reverse Mortgages" by Tara Coates (www.aarp.org/money/credit-loans-debt/ info-02-2011/10-questions-answered-about-reverse-mortgages .html).

Chapter 37: Kids Cost Money

The opening quote is from the article "Can You Really Afford That Second Child . . . and Does It Really Matter?" by Kate Ashford on MSN Money (http://money.bundle.com/article/can-you -really-afford-second-child-and-does-it-really-matter).

For statistics on the costs of child rearing, see "Expenditures on Children by Families, 2009," U.S. Department of Agriculture, Center for Nutrition Policy and Promotion, Miscellaneous Publication Number 1528-2009 (www.cnpp.usda.gov/Publications/CRC/crc2009.pdf).

If you're thinking of having one child, check out *Parenting an Only Child* and *The Case for the Only Child* by social psychologist Susan Newman.

See the article "America's Best, Affordable Places to Raise Kids" on Businessweek.com (www.businessweek.com/lifestyle/content/ dec2010/bw20101214_289257.htm).

For interesting views on helping—or rather *not* helping—your children pay for college, see "6 Reasons Not to Save for Kids' College" by Sally Herigstad, posted on December 7, 2009, on MSN Money (http://money.bundle.com/article/AssetsCollege-Savings6 -reasons-save-kids-college-7284).

"An Introduction to 529 Plans: The Good, the Bad and the Inconsequential" at Scholarships.com provides a good overview of these state-by-state plans (www.scholarships.com/financial -aid/college-savings-accounts/an-introduction-to-529-plans-the -good-the-bad-and-the-inconsequential).

For resources that can help you raise financially responsible children, see *Raising Financially Fit Kids* by Joline Godfrey, founder of Independent Means Inc., and visit her website (http://indepen dentmeans.com).

Chapter 38: Giving Back

Good sources of statistics and general information on U.S. giving include the National Philanthropic Trust (www.nptrust.org), the Urban Institute's National Center for Charitable Statistics (http://nccs.urban.org), and Giving USA (http://givingusa.org).

The example in the table was constructed from information at Vanguard's website Vanguard Charitable Endowment Program—Tax Benefits (https://www.vanguardcharitable.org/giving/tax _benefits_donor_advised_funds.html).

Also see the Vanguard guide "How to Value Your Contribution for Tax Purposes" at the Vanguard website (https://a248.e.akamai .net/f/248/21630/7d/im.uprinv.com/rc/sr2/vcep/howtovalue contributionfortax.pdf).

For more information on gift annuities, visit the American Council on Gift Annuities website (www.acga-web.org).

Also see the New York State Insurance Department's page listing the top 10 questions about the charitable gift annuity (www .ins.state.ny.us/que_top10/que_life_cha.htm).

Chapter 39: In Sickness and in Wealth

The figures on nursing home costs are from retirementincome journal.com, April 27, 2011 (http://retirementincomejournal.com/issue/april-27-2011/article/average-annual-cost-of-private -nursing-home-room-85-775).

Other data and statistics come from seniorlaw.com (http://seniorlaw.com/medicare.htm) and from the PHI blog, *PolicyWorks* (http://phinational.org/archives/costs-for-home-health-aide -services-remain-unchanged).

The quote from Scott J. Witt of Witt Actuarial Services is from an interview with him on March 2, 2011.

The October 16, 2010, *Wall Street Journal* article "Long-Term-Care Premiums Soar" by Anne Tergesen and Leslie Scism reported that John Hancock was seeking a 40% increase in premiums on about 850,000 of its 1.1 million policyholders.

Also see the National Clearinghouse for Long-Term Care Information (www.longtermcare.gov). This site provides solid resources for planning for long-term care, including a long-term care calculator for figuring how much money you would need to save to pay for your own care (in the "Planning Steps" section).

The article "Medigap: Your Supplemental Insurance" at AARP provides a good overview and links to resources on Medigap insurance (www.aarp.org/health/medicare-insurance/info-01-2011/understanding_medicare_medigap.html).

Chapter 40: Estate Planning Basics

James (Jay) Hughes is the author of *Family Wealth: Keeping It in the Family*, from which the opening quote is drawn. Hughes is a leading thinker and practitioner in helping families preserve their wealth across generations by addressing potentially negative consequences of financial success. For a self-education in wills, living trusts, and estate planning considerations, access the site of legal information publisher Nolo (www.nolo.com/legal-encyclopedia/wills-trusts-estates).

Plan Your Estate (Nolo, 2010) by attorney Denis Clifford is an excellent book of estate planning considerations and tools.

Also, the website of AARP is a solid resource (www.aarp.org/money/estate-planning). I don't recommend do-it-yourself estate planning, which AARP sometimes endorses.

See my July 13, 2010, article "The Secret Your Estate Planning Lawyer Won't Tell You" at the *Huffington Post* for more details on using a directed trustee (www.huffingtonpost.com/dan-solin/the-secret-your-estate-pl_b_642539.html).

Glossary

Actively managed fund: Mutual funds where the fund managers rely on research and their judgment to buy and sell securities with the aim of beating a designated benchmark, like the S&P 500 index.

Actuary: An expert in making calculations related to insurance life expectancy, premiums, benefits, policy features, and reserves needed to pay benefits.

Adjustable-rate mortgage (ARM): Mortgage with a rate tied to a widely published interest rate, such as the prime rate, usually with points added. The rate can adjust every one, two, three, or five years.

Alternative investments: Asset classes other than stocks and bonds, bank deposits, treasuries, mutual funds, and real estate. They include gold, commodities, stock options, and venture capital and hedge funds, among others.

Annuity: Contract sold by insurance companies that provides for a lump-sum payment or stream of payments. Annuities can be fixed or variable. They feature tax deferral.

Asset: In investing, a possession that earns dividends or interest and/or appreciates in price and/or can be sold for cash. In accounting, cash, accounts receivables, inventory, property, and other items that can earn money or be sold are considered assets.

Asset allocation: The process of dividing your investments among stocks, bonds, and cash to match investment goals, risk tolerance, and time horizon.

Automatic savings plan: Having an amount deducted regularly from a paycheck or an account on specific dates and transferred to a savings or money market account.

Baby boomer: According to the U.S. Census Bureau, an American born between January 1, 1946, and December 31, 1964.

Balance sheet: A financial statement that lists the assets, liabilities, and net worth of an organization, household, or individual.

Bankruptcy: A court-supervised process of having certain debts legally wiped out due to inability to pay. Also, reorganization or liquidation of an insolvent company.

Bear market: A period of sustained decreases in overall stock prices. A downturn of 20% over a few months is one common measure.

Bond: Debt instruments issued by companies or governments to raise capital by borrowing. The issuer of the bond promises to repay the principal with interest on a specific date.

Bond rating: A published evaluation of the risk of a bond, based on the issuer's creditworthiness and likelihood of default. Bond ratings determine the interest rate the issuer will pay on the bond.

Budget: Allocating income and other inflows of cash to expenses, usually over a month, quarter, or year.

Bull market: A period of sustained increases in overall stock prices, particularly compared with normal long-term appreciation.

Capital gains: Appreciation in the price or value of an asset, such as securities or real estate. Capital gains are generally "realized" when the asset is sold. Until then they are referred to as "paper gains."

Capital gains tax: A tax on realized capital gains. Generally, the U.S. capital gains tax rate has been lower than the average income tax.

Capitalization: The number of shares a company has outstanding in the market multiplied by the price per share. Also known as market cap, or market capitalization.

Cash drag: Lagging performance of an index fund (compared with its index) due to part of the fund being in cash or cash equivalents.

Cash equivalent: Financial instruments safe enough to be considered cash, usually money market funds and U.S. Treasury bills.

Cash value life insurance: Whole life and universal life insurance policies, which accrue cash value over the policy term because part of the premium is invested.

Certificate of deposit (CD): An interest-bearing deposit with a bank for a specific period, such as six months or one, two, three, or five years, with penalties for early withdrawal. They are sold to consumers and usually insured by the FDIC.

Charitable organization: A qualifying charity as defined in section 501(c)(3) of the U.S. tax code. Donations to these organizations are generally tax deductible.

Churning: A broker or investment adviser encouraging a customer to buy and sell to increase his or her commissions. The SEC and securities exchanges forbid churning.

College accounts: Various tax-advantaged savings accounts and other plans that allow parents to accumulate money to pay for a child's higher education.

Coverage: In insurance, the benefit the insurer will pay under a policy, either for a specific event (such as death) or total payout (such as health-care expenses in a year).

Credit counselor: Adviser to distressed debtors who is recognized by creditors as negotiating on behalf of debtors. Many unscrupulous people pose as credit counselors, so visit the National Foundation for Credit Counseling (www.nfcc.org) for reputable ones.

Credit report: Compilation of an individual's (or organization's) record of paying their loans. The three major U.S. credit bureaus are Equifax, Experian, and TransUnion.

Current value: The present value of an amount of money to be paid in the future, calculated by discounting that amount by an interest rate. Alternatively, it is the amount you'd have to invest today at that rate to have the future sum at the future date.

Cyclical recession: Pause in economic growth due to the periodic but unpredictable recurring mismatch between supply and demand that characterizes economies. Also known as the business cycle.

Day trading: Buying and selling a stock or other financial instrument within a single day. The vast majority of day traders lose all, or a significant portion, of their investments.

Death benefit: The amount to be paid to beneficiaries of a life insurance policy if the policyholder dies. Also known as the coverage or the policy's face amount.

Debt management plan: An arrangement negotiated by a credit counseling agency where a distressed debtor pays an amount to the agency, which then pays the creditors. These plans aim to reduce, forgive, or stretch out payments.

Disclosure: The practice of public companies sharing data on financial performance, operations, and risks with investors so they can make informed decisions. Audited financial statements and SEC filings are common forms of disclosure.

Diversified: Investments selected to represent a variety of asset classes or industries, or a broad range of securities in an asset class, to spread or lower the risk of the portfolio.

Dollar-cost averaging: A system of investing a fixed dollar amount in shares of a stock or fund at a regular interval. The goal is to buy more shares when the price is low and obtain a lower average price than if you bought a set number of shares at each interval.

Efficient markets theory: The idea that efforts to beat the market are futile because all facts that may affect the market's valuation of stocks are factored into its price.

Estate tax: Federal or state taxes levied on the amount of assets in an estate. U.S. estate tax rates and the estate tax exclusion (assets not subject to the tax) have varied over time.

Exchange traded funds (ETFs): A security or mutual fund that tracks a designated index but is traded like a stock on an exchange and purchased and sold through brokers.

Executor: The person, named in a will, charged with seeing that the terms of the will are carried out.

Expected returns: The projected future returns on an investment, modified by a factor that accounts for the risk of those returns.

Expense ratio: The ratio of operating expenses and management fees (paid by the investors) to the total amount invested in a fund. Lower expense ratios tend to correlate positively with higher returns.

Fee-only adviser: Advisers and financial planners who derive none of their income from commissions from, or arrangements with, financial institutions or anyone other than their clients.

Fiduciary: An investment adviser who is required to act solely in the client's best interest. Brokers are *not* fiduciaries. All Registered Investment Advisors are fiduciaries.

Financial planner: Person representing themselves as prepared to help people achieve financial goals but who vary in their knowledge, expertise, qualifications, and motives. Many financial planners are salespeople for financial institutions and insurance companies who have inherent conflicts of interest when they recommend strategies or products.

Fixed-income investments: Investments that pay a fixed rate of return, usually corporate or government bonds or funds that invest in them.

Foreclosure: Legal process where a lender takes possession of a home of a homeowner who has fallen behind on their mortgage payments.

Fund family: A mutual fund company that offers a range of funds with varying levels of risk and return to suit investors ranging from conservative to aggressive.

Growth stocks: Stocks that have significant earnings and growth rates well in excess of that of the overall economy. They typically pay no dividends because they reinvest all earnings in the company.

Health maintenance organization (HMO): Originally, organizations of salaried caregivers in brick-and-mortar institutions, but now usually networks of providers similar to a preferred provider organization (PPO). HMOs usually require the selection of a primary care physician who manages your healthcare.

Hedge fund: A fund set up as a private partnership (to avoid regulation) to invest in speculative instruments, with high minimum investments, high fees, and restrictions on withdrawals.

House fund: A mutual fund sponsored by or assembled by a brokerage house and usually carrying the name of the house, such as the Merrill Lynch Aggressive Growth Fund.

Hyperactive investing: A term I coined in *The Smartest Investment Book You'll Ever Read* to refer to the excessive trading and costs in actively managed mutual funds. This excessive activity increases costs and reduces returns.

Index: A statistical economic or financial measure constructed of specific components, like the consumer price index and its basket of goods and services or a stock index composed of selected stocks, like the Dow Jones Industrial Average or the S&P 500 index.

Index fund: A mutual fund that tracks a recognized market index, such as the Standard & Poor's 500 index or the Russell 2000 index.

Individual retirement account (IRA): A tax-deferred retirement account that allows an employee to make tax-deductible contributions to up to a maximum annual amount. Taxes on the principal and accumulated earnings are due upon withdrawal, but you *must* start withdrawals shortly after reaching age 70½.

Inflation: Erosion of the purchasing power of a currency, usually due to rising prices in an economy. Two measures of inflation in the United States are the Consumer Price Index (CPI) and the Producer Price Index (PPI).

Initial public offering (IPO): A stock being offered for sale to the public for the first time.

Insider trading: Buying or selling a security based on information that has not been released to the public (inside information). An insider is usually defined as an officer, director, or key employee, but can include family members or others. Insider trading is illegal.

Insolvency: The inability of a person or organization to pay financial obligations as they become due.

Investment bank: A company that underwrites and distributes securities for companies raising money in the capital markets. They also invest in securities for their own account with the goal of earning returns.

Investment company: A company that pools funds from investors and invests them in securities in exchange for a management fee, usually charged as a percent of the assets under management for each customer.

Investment horizon: The period that you intend to hold an investment or years until you intend to liquidate an asset or a portfolio.

Large-cap stocks: Short for large-capitalization stocks. Stocks of companies with a market capitalization above $10 billion (or above $8 billion by some definitions).

Liabilities: Money or debts owed to another person or entity, including loans, taxes, and judgments.

Liquid assets: Assets that can be readily sold and converted to cash, such as publicly traded stocks.

Liquidation: Closing down a company and selling off its assets, either voluntarily or through involuntary bankruptcy.

Liquidity: Having cash (or cash equivalents) to spend or to pay liabilities as they become due. Publicly traded stocks are more liquid than a house because they can be sold faster.

Load: Sales commission paid by investors in a mutual fund that charges commissions. A fund that doesn't charge them is a no-load fund.

Load fund: A mutual fund that carries a sales charge to compensate the broker or sales representative selling it. A no-load fund carries no such charge. The rationale for the charge is that the broker or sales representative explains the fund and provides related advice.

Management buyout: A transaction in which the management of a company buys it from the shareholders, often with loans secured by the company's assets as part of the funding.

Marginal income tax rate: The tax rate applied to an additional dollar of income. The tax bracket that applies to additional income for an individual.

Market inefficiencies: Behavior by investors and sellers of securities that can generate inaccurate securities prices, including issuing inaccurate financial statements and insider trading.

Medigap insurance: Insurance for benefits to cover healthcare costs not covered by Medicare.

Mid-cap stocks: Short for middle-capitalization stocks. Stocks of companies with a market capitalization between $2 billion and $10 billion (or between $4 billion and $8 billion by some definitions).

Money market fund: Mutual funds that pay interest to shareholders and aim to maintain a net asset value of $1 a share. They typically invest in short-term, high-quality, liquid debt.

Monte Carlo analysis: Analysis of various potential outcomes (or scenarios) based on repeated trials with various factors assigned various probabilities.

Mortgage: Loan used to buy a home or commercial property, secured by the property.

Mortgage-backed securities: Bonds created by bundling the future payments of interest and principal from thousands of individual mortgages into a single security in a process called securitization.

Mutual fund: Arrangement in which investment professionals accept money from the public, pool the money into a fund with specific investment objectives, and manage the fund and administrative details. Mutual funds invest in a wide range of securities and may be either actively or passively managed.

Net worth: Value of the assets of a person, business, or other entity minus the value of their liabilities.

No-load fund: A mutual fund that does not carry a sales charge to compensate the broker or sales representative selling it.

Passively managed fund: A fund in which the fund manager aims to mirror the performance of a market index.

Penny stock: Highly speculative stocks of small companies not traded on major stock exchanges.

Performance drag: Failure of an index fund to equal the performance of its index, due to the fund not precisely tracking the composition of the index.

Planned giving: Charitable donations arranged during the donor's lifetime, usually with tax benefits and often using annuities or trusts.

Portfolio: A combination of securities or other assets designed to reduce risk or achieve a specific level of risk.

Portfolio theory: Area of academic finance that quantifies expected risks and returns of securities and funds to allocate assets to produce the best return for a given level of risk.

Preferred provider organization (PPO): A network of healthcare providers assembled by an insurer who negotiates with the providers for fees for services delivered to insured individuals. PPOs typically permit insured individuals to go out of network, usually with a referral and often at higher cost.

Public company: A company registered with the Securities and Exchange Commission (SEC) for the purpose of raising capital from the investing public.

Rating agency: An organization that evaluates the risk of corporate and government bonds to assist the market in pricing them. The three main U.S. rating agencies are Standard & Poor's, Moody's Investor Services, and Fitch Ratings.

Rebalancing: The process of returning the asset allocations in a portfolio to the desired percentages after they have changed (due to increases or decreases in asset values) or when the investor's situation has changed.

Registered Investment Advisor (RIA): An adviser registered with the Securities and Exchange Commission and who manages investment funds for clients. An RIA is considered a fiduciary.

Risk capacity: An investor's ability to absorb losses in asset value or variability of returns without suffering longer-term financial harm.

Risk-return profile: The tradeoff between risk and return in an investment or portfolio. The return achievable for a given level of risk.

Risk tolerance: An investor's emotional or financial ability to tolerate losses in asset value or variability of returns in exchange for potentially higher returns.

Roth IRA (Individual Retirement Account): An IRA for which contributions are made out of after-tax income. It works like a regular IRA, except contributions are not tax deductible and distributions are generally tax free.

Securities and Exchange Commission (SEC): The chief regulatory body of the U.S. capital markets and public companies. The SEC as currently structured was created in 1934 during the Great Depression.

Short sale: In real estate, sale of a home for less than the amount owed on the mortgage, with the approval of the bank that holds the mortgage.

Small-cap stocks: Short for small-capitalization stocks. Stocks of companies with a market capitalization of less than $2 billion (or less than $4 billion by some definitions).

Standard deviation: A statistical measure of risk—specifically, the historical volatility of a stock, mutual fund, or portfolio. It measures the year-to-year deviation of the stock's, fund's, or portfolio's returns from its average annual return; it's usually expressed as an annualized number. The higher the standard deviation, the higher the risk of the investment.

Stop-loss: Regarding healthcare insurance, the maximum amount the insured will have to pay to providers out of pocket during a period (usually a year).

Subprime mortgages: Loans to borrowers with low credit scores. Also, mortgage loans that do not meet the usual criteria set by Fannie Mae and Freddie Mac.

Tax-deferred account: An investment on which returns are not taxed until they are withdrawn from the account. Traditional IRAs and 401(k) plans are the most common tax-deferred investments.

Tax efficient: An investment that minimizes the taxes paid on the earnings to maximize the amount on which returns can be earned. Index funds are very tax efficient. Most actively managed funds are not.

Tax loss harvesting: Selling securities at a loss and using the loss to offset future capital gains tax liability.

Term life insurance: Insurance that pays a death benefit of a specific amount during the life (or term) of the policy, which is generally 10, 20, or 30 years. Term insurance accrues no cash value. When the policy expires, so does the coverage.

Treasury securities: Securities issued by the U.S. Treasury of various maturities and sold to investors to fund the federal debt.

Trust: Legal agreement in which a party (the grantor) places ownership of assets under the control of another party (the trustee) for the benefit of a third party (the beneficiary). There are many different types of trusts designed for different purposes.

Underwater: In real estate, a situation where a homeowner owes more on their mortgage than they could sell the house for in the current market.

Universal life insurance: Cash value life insurance that does not pay a guaranteed death benefit, but allows more flexible premium payments (than whole life) because the policyholder can choose how much to contribute to the investment component. Premiums are automatically deducted from the cash value if you miss your payments. You have no control over the investment component unless it's a variable policy, in which the insurer offers different investment options.

Value stocks: Stocks considered to be undervalued in price relative to their underlying fundamentals, like book value, sales, and earnings.

Variability: The possible range of outcomes for a stock, fund, or portfolio.

Vested assets: A person's right to the full amount of a designated benefit, like a 401(k) plan, regardless of whether he or she remains an employee of the company sponsoring the plan.

Whole life insurance: Cash value life insurance that pays a guaranteed death benefit for the life of the policyholder (as long as the premiums are paid as agreed). Premiums are level for a set period, often for life, and the policyholder does not control the investment component. Dividends may be used to increase the cash value or to reduce annual premiums.

Will: A legal document that directs the executor of an individual's estate on how assets should be distributed and how other final wishes, such as funeral arrangements, should be carried out.

APPENDIX

Risk and Return Summaries

The following pages feature three simulated index model portfolios from Vanguard, Fidelity, and T. Rowe Price that show the hypothetical results of five risk levels: low risk (20% stocks/80% bonds), medium-low risk (40% stocks/60% bonds), medium risk (60% stocks/40% bonds), medium-high risk (80% stocks/20% bonds), and high risk (100% stocks/0% bonds).

The following charts provide the composition of the respective model portfolios and the summary of raw data used to create simulated index performance numbers. The *average annualized return* (geometric) reflects the performance results of the portfolios referenced. The *annualized standard deviation* is a statistical measure of the historical volatility of the portfolios referenced.

In developing the data, in those instances where actual fund data were not available for the entire period, appropriate market indexes were used to approximate the yearly returns of the funds. Each index used is identified. A fee was then subtracted from the returns of each index to account for the expense ratios of funds that track the index.

The data for all portfolios are for the period 1991–2010.

VANGUARD FUNDS

Vanguard funds used are the Vanguard Total Stock Market Index Fund (VTSMX), the Vanguard Total International Stock Market Index Fund (VGTSX), and the Vanguard Total Bond Market Index Fund (VBMFX). The following chart provides the disposition of the funds at five risk levels:

Fund	Low Risk	Medium-Low Risk	Medium Risk	Medium-High Risk	High Risk
VTSMX	14%	28%	42%	56%	70%
VGTSX	6%	12%	18%	24%	30%
VBMFX	80%	60%	40%	20%	0%

Risk and Return

VANGUARD FUNDS: RISK AND RETURN 20 YEARS

All performance data are expressed in percent and are hypothetical investment results over the period 1991–2010:

Measure	Low Risk	Medium-Low Risk	Medium Risk	Medium-High Risk	High Risk
Average annual return (geometric)	7.39	7.95	8.36	8.61	8.66
Annualized standard deviation	5.64	8.34	11.69	15.27	18.95
Worst single-calendar-year period	−3.79	−12.63	−21.47	−30.32	−39.16
Worst two-calendar-year period	3.17	−6.04	−15.30	−24.61	−33.99
Worst three-calendar-year period	10.58	−1.21	−15.03	−27.51	−38.71

Raw Data

Here are the raw data used to produce the risk and return data for the Vanguard Fund portfolios:

VTSMX	Actual fund returns 1993–2010 (Wilshire 5000 Index: −0.25% per year 1991–1992)
VGTSX	Actual fund returns 1997–2010 (MSCI EAFE Index: −0.35% per year 1991–1996)
VBMFX	Actual fund returns 1991–2010

FIDELITY FUNDS

Fidelity funds used are the Fidelity Spartan Total Market Index Fund (FSTMX), the Fidelity Spartan International Index Fund (FSIIX), and the Fidelity Spartan U.S. Bond Index Fund (FBIDX). The following chart provides the disposition of the funds at five risk levels:

Fund	Low Risk	Medium- Low Risk	Medium Risk	Medium- High Risk	High Risk
FSTMX	14%	28%	42%	56%	70%
FSIIX	6%	12%	18%	24%	30%
FBIDX	80%	60%	40%	20%	0%

Risk and Return

FIDELITY FUNDS: RISK AND RETURN 20 YEARS

All performance data are expressed in percent and are hypothetical
investment results over the period 1991–2010:

Measure	Low Risk	Medium-Low Risk	Medium Risk	Medium-High Risk	High Risk
Average annual return (geometric)	7.44	7.94	8.30	8.50	8.51
Annualized standard deviation	5.86	8.46	11.71	15.20	18. 81
Worst single-calendar-year period	−4.68	−13.13	−21.57	−30.01	−38.46
Worst two-calendar-year period	0.79	−7.84	−16.53	−25.27	−34.08
Worst three-calendar-year period	8.08	−0.50	−14.82	−27.71	−39.24

Raw Data

Here are the raw data used to produce the risk and return data
for the Fidelity Fund portfolios:

FSTMX	Actual fund returns 1998–2010 (Wilshire 5000 Index: −0.25% per year 1991–1997)
FSIIX	Actual fund returns 1998–2010 (MSCI EAFE Index: −0.35% per year 1991–1997)
FBIDX	Actual fund returns 1991–2010

T. ROWE PRICE FUNDS

T. Rowe Price funds used are the T. Rowe Price Total Equity Market Fund (POMIX), the T. Rowe Price International Equity Index Fund (PIEQX), and the T. Rowe Price U.S. Bond Index Fund (PBDIX). The following chart shows the allocation of the funds at five risk levels:

Fund	Low Risk	Medium-Low Risk	Medium Risk	Medium-High Risk	High Risk
POMIX	14%	28%	42%	56%	70%
PIEQX	6%	12%	18%	24%	30%
PBDIX	80%	60%	40%	20%	0%

Risk and Return

T. ROWE PRICE FUNDS: RISK AND RETURN 20 YEARS

All performance data are expressed in percent and are hypothetical investment results over the period 1991–2010:

Measure	Low Risk	Medium-Low Risk	Medium Risk	Medium-High Risk	High Risk
Average annual return (geometric)	6.86	7.30	7.59	7.72	7.66
Annualized standard deviation	5.72	8.33	11.61	15.13	18.76
Worst single-calendar-year period	−3.40	−12.25	−21.09	−29.94	−38.78
Worst two-calendar-year period	3.22	−6.15	−15.54	−24.95	−34.37
Worst three-calendar-year period	10.29	−1.28	−15.15	−27.66	−38.90

Raw Data

Here are the raw data used to produce the risk and return data for the T. Rowe Price Fund portfolios:

POMIX	Actual fund returns 1999–2010 (Wilshire 5000 Index: −0.40% per year 1991–1998)
PIEQX	Actual fund returns 2001–2010 (MSCI EAFE Index: −0.50% per year 1991–2000)
PBDIX	Actual fund returns 2001–2010 (Lehman [now Barclays] Aggregate Bond Index: −0.30% per year 1991–2000)

Acknowledgments

I benefited greatly (as I always do) from the insights of John Duff, my publisher at Perigee Books.

My literary agent, Andrea Barzvi, at International Creative Management, has been a continuing source of support and guidance.

I could not have written this book without the assistance of Tom Gorman, an MBA and distinguished author of many valuable books on a variety of business, management, and financial topics.

I relied heavily for some of the insurance information on Scott Witt, a fee-only insurance adviser (wittactuarialservices.com). His insight and expertise were immensely helpful.

It's one thing to write a book and quite another to publicize and distribute it to a wide audience. I am fortunate to have the assistance of Patrick Nolan and the able sales team at Penguin; Elizabeth Hanslik Psaltis, marketing director; and Heather Connor, senior publicist. Their expertise, enthusiasm, and tireless efforts have contributed immeasurably to the success of the Smartest series of books.

Sean Kelly, of Kelly & Associates, investment advisers and consultants, provided me with risk and return data and very helpful comments on the manuscript.

My wife, Patricia Solin, patiently reviews all my books, including this one, and tolerates living with me while I am writing them.

Publisher's Note

This publication contains the opinions and ideas of its author. It is intended to provide helpful and informative material on the subject matter covered. It is sold with the understanding that the author and publisher are not engaged in rendering professional services in the book. If the reader requires personal assistance or advice, a competent professional should be consulted. The author and publisher specifically disclaim any responsibility for any liability, loss, or risk, personal or otherwise, which is incurred as a consequence, directly or indirectly, of the use and application of any of the contents of this book.

Trademarks: All terms mentioned in this book that are known to be or are suspected of being trademarks or service marks have been appropriately capitalized. Perigee Books cannot attest to the accuracy of this information. Use of a term in this book should not be regarded as affecting the validity of any trademark or service mark.

Legal disclaimer: This book provides general information that is intended, but not guaranteed, to be correct and up-to-date. The information is not presented as a source of investment, tax, or legal advice. You should not rely on statements or representations made within the book or by any externally referenced sources. If you need investment, tax, or legal advice upon which you intend to rely in the course of your financial, business, or legal affairs, consult a competent, independent financial adviser, accountant, or attorney.

The contents of this book should not be taken as financial or legal advice, or as an offer to buy or sell any securities, fund, type of fund, or financial instruments. It should not be taken as an endorsement or recommendation of any particular company or individual, and no responsibility can be taken for inaccuracies, omissions, or errors. The information presented is not to be considered investment or legal advice. The reader should consult a Registered Investment Advisor or registered dealer or attorney prior to making any investment or legal decision.

The author does not assume any responsibility for actions or non-actions taken by people who have read this book, and no one shall be entitled to a claim for detrimental reliance based upon any information provided or expressed herein. Your use of any information provided herein does not constitute any type of contractual relationship between yourself and the provider(s) of this information. The author hereby disclaims all responsibility and liability for all use of any information provided in this book.

The materials here are not to be interpreted as establishing an attorney-client or any other relationship between the reader and the author or his firm.

Although great effort has been expended to ensure that only the most meaningful resources are referenced in these pages, the author does not endorse, guarantee, or warranty the accuracy, reliability, or thoroughness of any referenced information, product, or service. Any opinions, advice, statements, services, offers, or other information or content expressed or made available by third parties are those of the author(s) or publisher(s) alone. Reference to other sources of information does not constitute a referral, endorsement, or recommendation of any product or service. The existence of any particular reference is simply intended to imply potential interest to the reader.

The views expressed herein are exclusively those of the author and do not represent the views of any other person or any organization with which the author is, or may be, associated.

Index

Page numbers in **bold** indicate tables.